FINDING
STRENGTH
IN
TOUGH
TIMES

A Biblical Approach *for* Conquering Life's Hardships

RON WAGLEY

RM RUSSELL MEDIA

Boise, Idaho

If you unexpectedly found yourself lying in a hospital bed with medical personnel busily working all about you, Ron Wagley is the person you would want to see walking through the door. He brings a profound sense of peace, wisdom, and unshakeable trust in God wherever he goes. After he visited with you, you would know everything was going to be OK. If you were in that hospital bed, you probably wouldn't be able to write down all the wisdom that he shared with you. Thankfully, you wouldn't have to. This book is a gift to everyone who has endured a difficult time in their life. Wagley's grasp of Scripture, common sense wisdom, and breadth of thought, makes this a go-to book whenever storm clouds begin gathering overhead.

DR. RICHARD BLACKABY, Co-author of *Experiencing God* and *Spiritual Leadership;* President of Blackaby Ministries International

No matter how insulated or comfortable we might be, we all experience hardship, crisis, and adversity. Making sense out of our circumstances can be challenging, and we may end up with more questions than answers. *Finding Strength in Tough Times* may or may not ease the immediate pain, but this skillfully written book does provide an incredibly helpful perspective and a number of very practical exercises. Whether we are experiencing adversity or hardship at the moment, we will. There's something here for all of us.

TIM IRWIN, Ph.D., Author of *Derailed, Ten Lessons Learned from Catastrophic Failures of Leadership.*

As a Biblical counselor, I will recommend *Finding Strength in Tough Times* to those going through difficult times, because it gives us God's perspective and practical wisdom in dealing with the trials that we all will face. It goes beyond the theoretical to practical steps to take when facing a difficulty or making a tough decision.

CONNIE LARSON, MA, NANC Certified Biblical Counselor
and Conference Speaker

Through his extensive experience mentoring and counseling individuals in both workplace and Bible study settings, Ron Wagley has developed a practical, Biblical approach to helping people deal with life's inevitable hardships. He doesn't duck the hard questions even seasoned believers may ask when life crashes down on them: Where did this come from? Is this really God's will? Does God even care? Along with solid Scriptural answers, Ron shows us how we can endure adversity and emerge victorious. I recommend *Finding Strength in Tough Times* to men and women at every age and stage of life.

DAVID "MAC" MCQUISTON, President/CEO, CEO Forum, Inc.

Outstanding! Ron has a wonderful conversational approach that brings Biblical principles to life. This book is a great and powerful resource to encourage and equip us to stand firm when the adversities of life hit us from all sides.

CATHY I. OLSON, President, *OK Get Over It* Women's Conferences

Ron Wagley is an appropriate individual to write a book on facing adversity. As the retired head of a major insurance corporation, he grasps the certainty of trials and hardships. He understands the irrationality of expecting an environment where nothing bad happens. His experience of teaching, mentoring and counseling provided valuable insight into the nature of adversity and the significant intersection it can place lives at delicate times and places. This work displays his keen analytical ability and desire to examine and understand spiritual and worldly matters to the maximum extent possible. The reader is rewarded with the result of his passion for insight and detail. In *Finding Strength in*

Tough Times: A Biblical Approach for Conquering Life's Hardships, Ron provides a Biblical perspective that helps understand the causes and effects of adversity along with helpful do's and don'ts when hardship arrives. This book offers clear insight and direction into living a life, not free of difficulty, but characterized by peace and joy in the midst of its presence.

LARRY COLLETT, Chairman, Cass Information Systems;
Recognized as a Forbes Best 200 Small Company

Finding Strength in Tough Times is not a collection of clichés. It is practical wisdom that has grown out of living a life of faith in the real world. I've had the privilege of knowing Ron both as a friend and mentor. He has lived these principles and has taught them to many young men who are learning how to live out their faith in the business world and in their families. You are going to find great wisdom in this book that will help you when you face your own personal hardships.

STEVE LARSON, Lead Pastor,
The Bridge Church, Newbury Park, California

Finding Strength in Tough Times is a most poignant and accurate guide for those struggling with adversity and also appropriate for all of us to strengthen our respective foundation for when hardships inevitably arrive. Wagley walks readers through Biblical principles with a sound perspective for viewing trials and adversity and emerging with understanding, hope, and helpful guidelines to follow when crisis strikes. This could not be more timely with so many impacted by economic challenges along with life's other hardships that create questions and seemingly complete chaos. A successful mentor in both his corporate and personal life, he draws upon experience in providing an understanding based upon the truth of God's Word, the Bible.

JIM DUFF, Corporate Officer and Men's Bible Study Leader

I have had the privilege of knowing Ron Wagley and his family for over 40 years. We have walked beside him through trials and sufferings as well as through worldly success and achievement. Wagley's book comes out of his own life and the hurts of others—others he has prayed with and for, others he has encouraged along the way, others who have needed all kinds of help, men he has discipled, children and grandchildren he has loved, family members he has honored, employees he has treated kindly and ethically—in other words, people. This work will be a remarkable tool to bring hope to those who are suffering, thus fulfilling God's purpose for their life--to know Christ better and to make Him known to others.

FRAN MARTIN, Women's Bible Study Leader,
Speaker and Disciple-Maker

Finding Strength in Tough Times is extremely powerful, comprehensive, and presents key Biblical truths and the hope a person needs when experiencing hardship. Drawing principles from God's Word, the reader gains an understanding of where trials possibly originate, and sees a loving God who is ever-present, engaged and caring. We learn of the effectiveness and purpose of prayer and the importance of remembering God's prior faithfulness. The reader is offered numerous practical examples that aid in understanding God's truth and promises in the midst of difficult circumstances. This work is a valuable resource for everyone.

KEVIN FITZPATRICK, Director of Sales, RFSmart, Inc.

Everyone experiences pain and hardship in life, but how do we face such trials with faith and confidence? *Finding Strength in Tough Times* is a blueprint for Christians to stay God-centered through life's most difficult challenges. Ron Wagley has written a masterpiece we all desperately need.

BILL BOYAJIAN, author of *Developing the Mind of a Leader*,
Bill Boyajian & Associates

Published in Boise, Idaho, by Russell Media
Web: http://www.russell-media.com
For information please email info@russell-media.com.
ISBN (print):   978-1-937-498-092
ISBN (e-book):   978-1-937-498-108

Cover and Text Design by Woohoo Ink, LLC

Printed in the United States of America

This book may be purchased in bulk for educational, business, ministry, or
promotional use.

Dedicated in loving memory to

Jerry and *Marchetta Strader*

God's instruments and master disciple-makers
who lived out 2 Timothy 2:2

And

The Friday Night Bible Study Gang

Bob & Fran Martin

Noel & Sandy Funderburk

Larry & Annabelle Harn

Joe & Linda Davis

Harold & Carol Wheat

A unique group of couples who joined a six-week
Bible Study that lasted five years,

and along the way experienced
God's life-changing intervention.

CONTENTS

CONTENTS

APPENDICES

Another book on hardships? Well—yes.

But please no more "baloney theology" as stated by one grieving father struggling to find meaning and help after losing his daughter in a random shooting. In his pain, he expressed the need for greater understanding when experiencing the hurt that often accompanies adversity and hardships, "… three points, a poem and singing verses of 'Victory in Jesus' is baloney theology!"

Necessity was my mother of invention in writing and developing this book. It is the accumulation of over forty years of experience in mentoring individuals and leading Bible studies. This includes counseling and dealing with various forms of difficulties and crisis, some severe. Searching for Biblical answers and an understandable and helpful godly viewpoint prompted the creation of this work.

This book avoids pat answers administered like aspirin. I've attempted to provide a layperson's framework that addresses questions about life's difficulties from a Biblical perspective. The views and lessons included are for those who have experienced and will experience times when their roofs crash down. During such times, and in the midst of picking up the pieces, we don't need a lesson in theology, but we do crave answers. My aim also is to provide encouragement for dealing with and preparing for life's hardships.

Hardships come in different forms and levels of intensity. They demand attention and answers. Some bring pain or broken hearts. For many, such times frequently raise questions that refuse to go away or be ignored. Depending upon the severity, minds scream and run wild with unanswered questions of why is this happening; where did this come from; who caused this; and then, typically, why me. Core spiritual beliefs are no longer academic and may be fragile if only based on some nice-sounding religious cliché or vaguely remembered Sunday sermon.

My life, with its share of hardships, parallels the lives of many others. Be assured that by no means do I consider myself in the company and special category of survivors of extreme suffering caused by heart-breaking crisis. Many are included in the pages that follow. They are decorated heroes that wear the scars of catastrophe and deserve much praise for their endurance in advancing the cause of Christ through their enduring witness.

The fact that you've chosen to read or even scan through this book suggests some degree of interest, curiosity, or just plain desperation. Aside from wondering what this book is all about, you may question its relevance or value in your own life.

Let me offer some help as you decide whether to go further.

Finding Strength in Tough Times is an attempt to describe those unannounced and often painful life situations that are categorically grouped together as hardships. Admittedly, this is far too broad a term. What appears to be a hardship for one may be a minor inconvenience to another. Likewise, simply labeling an extreme crisis as a hardship falls short of and is inadequate of capturing in the suffering brought about by catastrophic life events.

Those in the mental health field have attempted to inventory and assign stress ratings to life events. At the high end are situations arising from death, divorce, health changes, job loss, and other extreme events. The other end of the scale includes family squabbles, stressful work conditions, difficult relationships, disappointments, and many others we all deal with during our lifetime.

Such scales have their place, but experience reveals that reactions to difficult events don't always validate the predicted level of stress. We've all seen and been amazed at folks who experience crisis victoriously; we also have been surprised when the smallest difficulty completely derails and incapacitates others.

Even though hardships come in different forms and levels of intensity, they do have several things in common. They all get attention; each is disruptive and at a minimum requires action or change. Some are inconvenient; however many bring pain and broken hearts that can shake our spiritual foundation. Some questions refuse to go away or be ignored.

Hardships have no limits and come regardless of who you are—Christian or non-Christian. Jesus taught in Matthew 5:45 that He [God] sends rain on the just and unjust alike." This confirms what we know from experience: As Christians, we have no supernatural umbrella shielding us from adversity. While we may acknowledge this truth, it typically comes as a surprise when our life takes a misstep and hardship inevitably arrives.

There are things we can and should do to prevent certain types of hardships, but the truth of life is that we will experience them.

Difficult times can wound and leave scars in our lives. The healing process is most often related to our reaction and viewpoint. For many when faced with crisis, their first thought is "Why did God allow this to happen? He couldn't possibly want this for me. This can't be His will." If continued, this line of thinking leads downhill to errant and irrational conclusions questioning God's love, His presence, or ignoring any "good" that can result from hardship.

There ought to be something radically different about a Christian's view and response. It's been said that if our Christian faith makes no difference in the things that make a difference, then what's the difference? The difference-maker is a perspective based upon the truths in the Bible. This prepares us for times of adversity. We may not be able to avoid them, but we can build a strong foundation to enable us to endure life's hardships and crises.

Don't misunderstand: this is not to say that the heartache that may accompany crisis will be replaced with some pious smile and false happiness. That denies the reality of the situation and masks the obvious presence of pain. What I am saying is that gaining a godly perspective and understanding with a sense of purpose provides enabling strength and encouragement to endure and emerge victorious.

It is my goal to present, in an understandable manner, Biblical truths that will create and strengthen our foundation to withstand the hardships of life. I have included suggestions regarding what to think, do, avoid, and believe during times of adversity. And, for maximum benefit, topics, Scripture references, and questions are provided for discussion with a small group.

Whether you're in the midst of a severe hardship and searching for answers, wanting to understand and gain a Biblical perspective, or seeking a resource for counseling others there is something for you.

With this in mind, *Finding Strength in Tough Times* is for all of us.

It is my prayer that this book will prove helpful and, if so, all the praise and glory must go to our wonderful Lord and Savior Jesus Christ. To Him be all the glory!

Those who love your instructions have great peace and do not stumble.

—PSALM 119:165

Finding Strength in Tough Times is written to provide hope and truth based upon God's Word, the Bible. The pages that follow talk about a God who is real and loves you more than you could ever imagine.

It is possible, however, that there will be those readers who do not know the God of the Bible and are hurting and searching for help and answers. And, while you may not know God, rest assured that He knows every detail about you. He desires to come into your life as your heavenly Father and have you partake of His love and presence as presented throughout this book.

CHAPTER ONE

HELP ME LORD…
MY ROOF JUST CRASHED!

R emember the last time your roof fell?

One minute all was well, and the next, you were reeling! Hurting. Questioning.

What is happening? Why?

Life's hardships are many. They cover a wide range of undesirable events and arrive in a variety of ways and levels of intensity. Some are extreme and arrive with a jolt. Others are less severe but still are unwelcome: whether a job loss, financial setback, family conflict—the list is long and varied.

Whatever we call them, crises, hardships, or simply inconveniences, we all have them. The Christian life does not include a manufacturer's warranty guaranteeing freedom from unwanted events. Unfortunately, there are those who go through life believing their Christianity provides such a guarantee. When adversity strikes—as it certainly will—this typically results in disappointment, or worse, disillusionment and possible tragedy.

Hardships are a very real part of life. Ecclesiastes 10:8-9 points out the risks of life, "When you dig a well, you might fall in. When you demolish an old wall, you could be bitten by a snake. When you work in a quarry, stones might fall and crush you. When you chop wood, there is danger with each stroke of your ax." Admittedly, there are preventative measures that could and should be taken; however, hardships and adversities will happen sometimes despite our best efforts.

Jesus, speaking of God, taught in His Sermon on the Mount in Matthew 5:45, "He gives his sunlight to both the evil and the good, and He sends rain on the just and the unjust alike." While the "sunlight" of good times and the "rain" of hardship falls upon Christians and non-Christians alike, the perspective and response from these two groups should be very different.

Making Sense Out of Life's Hardships

There are those seemingly more prepared to deal with hardships and the resulting difficulty and pain that adversity often inflicts. However, depending upon their severity, some situations challenge even the most faithful to endure and avoid lifelong suffering and grief. In those situations, roofs don't just fall, they crash; and often times with crippling results!

God's Word is not silent when it comes to the reality of hardships and suffering. The positive side is that trials can make our spiritual roofs stronger while moving us farther in the journey of developing the very character of Christ. God often uses crisis to help us discover His unlimited resources and presence at a new and deeper level.

Well-known pastor Rick Warren alluded to the presence and purpose of life's hardships in an interview when he responded to a question about his life since learning of his wife's cancer. "We were made by God, for God, and until you figure that out, life isn't going to make much sense. Life is a series of problems: Either you're in one now; you're just coming out of one; or you're getting ready to go into another one. The reason for this is that God is more interested in your character than your comfort. God is more interested in making your life holy than He is in making your life happy. We can be reasonably happy here on earth, but that's not the goal of life. The goal of life is to grow in character, in Christlikeness."[1]

This difficult truth was underscored when, as a nation, we were shocked with the senseless shooting in an Illinois church by a gunman who shot and killed a pastor in the midst of his Sunday sermon. The following week, this same grief-stricken church conducted a special service with an invited outside speaker. Few would ever understand the horror and pain except one that had experienced a similar tragedy. The guest speaker was the pastor of a Texas church similarly rampaged by a gunman. A decade earlier, this pastor's Texas church was horrified when a mentally deranged man barged into a youth prayer service cursing God and firing over a hundred rounds from a gun and exploding a pipe bomb leaving seven dead and seven wounded.

The visiting pastor brought a letter to be read to the Illinois church members from a father whose teenage daughter was among those killed. This father's emotional and heartfelt words describing his experience and perspective contain noteworthy lessons for all attempting to find meaning in such times of crisis.

This kind of tragedy is not something you get over with three points and a poem, a dose of Scripture, singing a verse of "Victory in Jesus" and a proclamation that "Everything's fine; let's move on." There's a Greek word for that kind of theology: baloney! Every day with Jesus is not sweeter than the day before. Some days are evil. In fact, the Bible says, "Stand that you might be able to stand in the evil day." [sic] Last Sunday was an evil day, and our hearts are breaking.

People are going to ask, "When are you going to get over this?" You're never going to get over this, but by God's grace you're going to get through it. And, God will give you joy and peace in the midst of it, in the midst of tears and heartache. Have you learned that? You are learning it now. It's the praise you give with a broken heart that is the greatest sacrifice you can offer to God.

The reality is that there is no way to avoid suffering. Thus, the critical test is whether believers can face trials and tribulations without sliding into despair. Far too many churches are fighting about the color of the carpet or the music they sing while suffering people keep looking for some sense of hope in this world and the next. It doesn't help that anyone with a TV remote can find scores of health and wealth boys who claim that true believers will avoid pain and strife altogether. God never promised us a life without trials.

As Americans, we want a carefree and happy life. We think that's God's will for our lives. Get a clue. God's will for your life is to make you into the image of his Son, and that only can happen through the heartaches and trials of life."[2]

Many of life's hardships painfully reveal and strengthen personal areas of weakness or needs that may require attention. Difficult times can challenge the sincerity or stability of our faith. Doubt may arise when attempting to make sense out of what is happening. None of these feelings or questions surprises God. He knows and will reveal Himself and respond like the loving Father He is.

This certainly was true for a Christian friend whose life took a turn that he never could have foreseen.

> I was raised in a Christian family and was very active in our church as a youth. The prayers of my parents and grandparents were that I would pursue the ministry as a preacher or become a missionary. It came as no surprise to my family and friends that I responded to God's calling to enter the ministry. My future was set as I graduated from seminary trained for pastoral service.
>
> I married soon following graduation and we had a baby daughter. Being a pastor and ministering was wonderful.

Little did I know that my life was going to come crashing down! During one of my pastor assignments, my wife announced that she no longer wanted to be a pastor's wife; she left and a divorce followed that included losing my daughter.

Devastation understates my feelings. My world crashed. I lost my wife and daughter. My church ministry and pastoral assignments ended. I felt ashamed and like a failure. My life goal was gone, and in my grief, I felt I had disappointed God. How could I face my family and friends? Everything I valued was lost.

I felt alone and, worse, didn't want to be with anyone out of embarrassment and shame. My heart ached and I can vividly remember spending endless nights on my knees crying and pouring my heart out to God. Everything seemed futile. I thought that my life had ended and felt God should take me and end my suffering and pain.

During the worst of this time, a Christian friend introduced me to a different secular career. Over time, I was able to influence others as a Christian living out my faith in a business environment. With my training, I was able to respond to others and help them via counseling. There were also times when I was able to lead Bible studies at work. God also brought a wonderful lady into my life who came from a similar situation. We were married and now together minister to those in our church.

I discovered that God's ways were far different than mine! My plans were disrupted and God graciously put the pieces of my life back together. My training and background were not wasted and opened up the door for a different kind of ministry. I came to realize that the life and testimony of a Christian layperson has as much, if not more, of a positive witness and influence than a paid professional preacher.

The pain and suffering that I experienced was terrible, but it wasn't the end. God is in the business of restoration. Looking back, I can see that the Good Shepherd cared for me as one of His wounded sheep. All was not lost and today I thank Him and rejoice for all He has done. He was always with me, even during those dark times when I didn't sense His presence; He never left and was working in me and had a wonderful plan for my future. I praise Him!

Another Christian related an amazing story. As a well-regarded Ph.D. and clinical microbiologist, he also ministers outside of his job in various domestic and international missions. Not only did his roof tumble down, but over time it brought his whole house with it! Yet in the midst of a series of surprising hardships, his foundation proved solid. He shared his family's experience of dealing with crisis.

I had taken time off and was in Brazil on a Christian mission. While there, I received a message that the hospital where I had worked for over 20 years had suddenly closed. And that wasn't the worst of it. I learned that my due back salary was lost. It was gone and our family's financial condition was strained. I came home to no job and little-to-no money.

Upon returning, and before I could begin to seek a new position, it was necessary to undergo previously scheduled corrective surgery. After the filing of my insurance claim, I received word that my health insurance premium would be doubled. This could not have come at a worse time! I had no job or income, our expenses were going up, and I had no prospects for work. Our bank account was dwindling and my job search was proving fruitless. If this wasn't enough, in the midst of this, we suffered the loss of my aged mother. Besides dealing with our grief, our finances suffered another setback with the additional funeral expense.

Coincidentally during this same time, I began to receive unsolicited calls from builders and attorneys seeking my expertise using my professional training. These were unexpected and thankfully provided some income flow.

Shortly after this, our family was shocked when my wife was diagnosed with breast cancer. Following surgery, she needed help in the days following each of her many treatments. Strangely, no calls for my consulting came during those difficult days after each of her treatments. However, when she got back on her feet, then I would once again receive consulting jobs, thus providing income. This pattern continued all during her treatments.

Hardships continued as we received notification that our health insurance would not pay for my wife's cancer treatments along with the unwelcome news that again our health insurance premium would be increased—indeed quadrupled from our original premium! We were faced with the significant expense of the treatments and could no longer pay the high premiums. Our bank account and other savings were gone and our health insurance coverage was going to lapse.

What was happening? I was serving God and lost my job, lost my income, my expenses were increasing, my mom died, my wife had cancer, our savings were exhausted, and I still was unemployed! When all appeared from the world's perspective to be lost, God intervened.

It was then that I received an unexpected call from a peer I had not talked to in well over thirty years. The conversation was short as he quickly asked me two questions: "How are you doing?" and "Do you want a job?" This materialized into a position with one of the most desirable companies in the U.S. with a salary and benefits better than what I had lost.

Each time when we had nothing—God provided. Our faith, trust, and thankfulness grew to new levels as we learned much about endurance during this time. We rested in and depended upon Him through all these trials. Our roof fell, but our foundation built upon God remained intact. We learned the value of building His firm foundation that is able to withstand life's most trying times and challenges.

Questioning Hardships

No doubt, when hardships arrive, they demand attention and answers. Depending upon the severity, adversity can leave you gasping for breath, reacting, and trying to figure out what's happening. If allowed, anxiety can be fueled by feelings of desperation and uncertainty. In our struggle to make sense out of the situation, questions arise which may include the big one: "Why me?" For many, suffering may cause an examination of their core beliefs wondering, "Who is God?" and "What do I really believe about Him?"

At such times, beliefs are no longer academic and may be fragile if limited or based on something recalled from a nice-sounding Sunday morning sermon. For many, bitterness creeps in with a hurting mindset that lashes out, "I don't deserve this and this is not fair." or "What kind of God would allow this to happen?"

Worse is when Christians react and direct their anger and questions toward God. "Why did You allow this to happen?" "Where are You?" "Do You even know or care what's happening?" "I've been a good Christian and You're not being fair." "Have all my efforts to live pure and right for You been worth it?" "I thought You loved me."

Chuck Colson said it well, "Life isn't like a book. Life isn't logical or sensible or orderly. Life is a mess most of the time. And theology must be lived out in the midst of that mess."[3]

The mess to which Colson refers includes trials and hardships that are not logical, defy being sensible, and, if allowed, can make a painful, heartbreaking mess out of our lives. We cannot conveniently compartmentalize our spirituality to Sunday mornings at church when dealing with and trying to understand life's struggles. This is only possible in a life immune from hardships.

Eugene Peterson commented on this outgrowth of adversity and suffering, "It (suffering) can be a means of grace, an instrument used by God by which we can cease floating passively on all manner of external attractions. It is by the grace of catastrophe that people sometimes come to themselves and see what is before them as if for the first time. Catastrophe can, like a mighty wind, blow away the abstract veil of theory and ideology and enable our own sovereign seeing."[4]

It may be that only through tough times will we discover what we actually believe about God, the truthfulness of who He is and discover personally His love, faithfulness, provision. It is here where the source of our trust and dependency is revealed.

Dependence vs. Independence

God created us to live in a relationship dependent upon Him as Lord and to bring Him glory at all times, even when challenged. "Bring all who claim Me as their God, for I have made them for My glory. It was I who created them" (Isaiah 43:7). We were created by and for God and His glory; it's not about us. We are to grow in our relationship with Him that includes trusting and relying upon Him during life's most challenging situations.

Many of life's struggles that crash into our lives causing pain and uncertainty test one of our basic natural human instincts— the desire to control and be independent. This is not unique and dates back to Adam's fall in the garden where Satan made his appeal, "you will be like God, knowing both good and evil." (Genesis 3:5) Adam chose to disobey God and assert his desire for independence and control by determining good and evil apart from God. Like Adam, many want or even need to control their lives and circumstances. Some relish their independence. Such an independent mindset reveals a source of confidence centered around self apart from God.

Independence conflicts with trust. Trusting in something outside of ourselves makes us dependent. God is purposeful and may use challenging circumstances to deal with such misplaced trust. Adversity can reveal the source of our dependence and strength. At such times, when our ability to control the situation is exhausted and proved inadequate, God is near and will reveal Himself and provide His sufficient strength and comfort. God responds well to the desperation that drives us to dependence on Him.

Where is God?

There may be times in the midst of a crisis when God appears to be distant. However, Scripture assures us that He is ever-present and responds to our searching and coming to Him. He is the Good Shepherd who cares for His sheep, particularly when wounded and suffering. The Psalms declare, "God is our refuge and strength, always ready to help in times of trouble" (Psalm 46:1). And later we are told, "Be still and know that I am God!" (Psalm 46:10).

When everything around us appears to be crashing, that may be the very time for stillness, solitude, and a seeking heart all of which enable God, through His Word, to speak and assure us of His presence and promises. We're not called to live our lives based upon God giving us reasons and justified explanations; we are to live trusting in Him.

We're not alone with our emotions and irrational thoughts during stressful times. Scripture is filled with mention of individuals who in the midst of adversity reacted and poured their hurt and pain out to God. Throughout the Psalms, David seems to shout to God his questions and raw emotions, "O Lord, how long will you forget me? Forever? How long will you look the other way? How long must I struggle with anguish in my soul, with sorrow in my heart every day?" (Psalm 13:1-2). "I cry out to God; yes, I shout. Oh, that God would listen to me!

When I was in deep trouble, I searched for the Lord. All night long I prayed with hands lifted toward heaven, but my soul was not comforted. I think of God, and I moan, overwhelmed with longing for His help. You don't let me sleep. I am too distressed even to pray" (Psalm 77:1-4).

It's important to note that in the midst of emotional distress, without exception throughout the book of Psalms, David concludes and is comforted in the truth that God is indeed engaged and in control even when David's feelings and anxieties run wild. We later see him comforted and at peace as he recites in this same Psalm God's blessings, "But then I recall all you have done, O Lord, I remember your wonderful deeds of long ago. They are constantly in my thoughts. I cannot stop thinking about your mighty works."

The Fickleness of Feelings

God's many truths as contained in the Bible are not conditioned or based upon our feelings or circumstances. Our thoughts and conclusions during times of pain and suffering can be flawed and even irrational. We must be sensitive and not allow our emotions take precedence over what we know is true (I can "know" God loves me; but I'm hurting so much that it doesn't "feel" like it; therefore God must not love me). While this may be understandable, God and Biblical truth should not be defined through the filter of feelings or circumstances; rather they should always be viewed through God's truth in the Bible. Trusting in and relying upon Biblical truth even when we don't feel like it during life's most pressing and painful moments is a sure sign of spiritual maturity.

Defining God on the basis of how we feel nullifies Scripture and defines truth through the subjective lens and criteria of human emotion. These can be manipulated by external circumstances and can change dramatically on any given day. As such, our feelings and emotions are suspect. They lie as often as they tell the truth. We must be extremely wary in accepting what they tell us about God. This is not to deny their presence; these feelings are real and normal. However, we must not allow them to govern our lives as we assess challenging situations. Truth overrules feelings and should govern behavior and beliefs based upon the truth of God's Word, the Bible.

A follower of Christ determines from the Bible alone what is true, and lives and trusts in it consistently rather than allowing circumstances or feelings to shape and determine reactions and conduct.

Comfort and perspective is found in knowing, and recalling the character of God as described in 1 John 3:20b, "God is greater than our feelings and He knows everything." The "everything" God knows includes understanding our pain and anguish. He also provides hope, supernatural strength, and peace during life's most trying times.

Isaiah 55:8-9 reminds us, "My thoughts are nothing like your thoughts, says the Lord. And, my ways are far beyond anything you could imagine. For just as the heavens are higher than the earth, so my ways are higher than your ways and my thoughts higher than your thoughts." Christians who expect God's thoughts and ways to comply with and reinforce their own are bound to be disillusioned. God cannot be commanded to perform as we wish, for our plans are not always His plans. I need to constantly remind myself that He's God and I'm not.

A.W. Tozer, Christian pastor and author, stated an essential truth about God, "God is what He is to Himself. He does not become what we believe. 'I Am that I Am.' We are on safe ground only when we know who and what kind of God He is and adjust our entire being to that holy concept."[5] Tozer continued, "It is of immense importance that our idea of God corresponds as nearly as possible to the true being of God."[6]

God is Purposeful

God wastes no experience to accomplish His plan for our lives.

It would be a mistake to conclude that God causes every hardship. He may cause or allow as He determines. What is true is that He can use any hardship and suffering for His purpose. In this regard, God is purposeful.

King Hezekiah's experience with God's discipline and testing provides one example of God's use of hardship. Second Chronicles 32:25-31 describes King Hezekiah as self-centered and proud. He excluded God and failed to honor Him, "Hezekiah did not respond appropriately to the kindness shown him and he became proud. So the Lord's anger came against him." God dealt with his prideful behavior by what was described as a "deathly illness." His critical condition led him to repent after which God restored his health. His sincerity was tested, "God withdrew from Hezekiah in order to test him and to see what was really in his heart." The king passed this final test of legitimacy and reigned until his death.

Like David and King Hezekiah, we may experience times of hardship designed to test our faith in the crucible of fire. Faith ranks high on God's list of priorities. Believing and trusting God when His purpose is not readily apparent or seen, and when questions are not answered is vital to a growing relationship with God. Resting on God's promises and his purpose cultivates our faith and dependence upon Him. God is interested less in our understanding than He is in our trust.

Branches, the Vine, and the Vine Keeper

In John 15, Jesus used the illustration of Himself as the vine, God as the vine keeper, and his children as branches. He says, "Yes, I am the vine; you are the branches. Those who remain in me, and I in them, will produce much fruit. For apart from me you can do nothing."

Using this analogy, when we as God's children experience stressful conditions, it is critical that we, like branches, stay connected to our life-giving source, Jesus the vine. By doing so, we can continue to bear fruit during challenging times. Jesus reminds us that apart from the vine (Jesus) "you can do nothing." Our feeble attempts to withstand and rise above our adversities in our own strength apart from Christ typically are damaging and fail. Jesus' message is clear: stay closely connected to Him.

God firmly establishes our connection to Him at the very moment we become a Christian. Unfortunately, we are prone to forget or even disregard the profound truth that when we become a Christian, God's Holy Spirit begins to reside in each of us. We oftentimes live our lives as if God is some distant being on call to be summoned when needed. The Apostle Paul tells us in Galatians 5:16, "So I say, let the Holy Spirit guide your lives. Then you won't be doing what your sinful nature craves." Later in verse 22-23a, he elaborates on the benefits of allowing God's Holy Spirit to do His good work in our lives, "But the Holy Spirit produces this kind of fruit in our lives: love, joy, peace, patience, kindness, goodness, faithfulness, gentleness, and self-control." Branches separated from the vine don't survive long; likewise, Christians who encounter hardship and attempt to cope by ignoring God typically respond in a worldly fashion. The fruit of joy is replaced by distress; peace with despair; patience reverts to anxiety; and self-control to desperation. Satan delights in such responses.

Outward signs of detached "branches" include hurting Christians who withdraw and may drop out of church and avoid fellowship with other believers; they typically no longer read the Bible, regard prayer as futile; become disillusioned and disenchanted, display bitterness and a critical spirit, and become ineffective and of little use to and for God. In contrast, times of disaster and suffering should be a stimulus for drawing nearer to fellow believers for support, while at the same time trusting in and seeking God's comfort and strength.

There can be no denying that God uses our experiences for His purposes in shaping our lives. However, it would be wrong to conclude that hardships and suffering always produce positive spiritual fruit. There is some truth in the maxim that going through a trying situation will leave you either better or bitter, but never the same. Much is dependent upon our perspective and our attitude toward Him.

As Richard and Henry Blackaby, well-known Christian authors, said in their book, *Spiritual Leadership*, "The key lies not in the experiences, whether good or bad, but in people's responses to those experiences. When some face hardships, they become bitter and fearful and quit trying. Others suffer similar setbacks, but choose to learn from their crisis and to become stronger for the experience."[7]

Jesus the Master Teacher

Despite what our emotions may be telling us during our hardships and we conjure up various irrational and negative thoughts and feelings, God is well aware of the situation. He loves His children and can be trusted as we continue to stay closely connected to Him. This is true even when we cannot understand or sense His presence.

At such times, we would do well to "Be still and know that I am God" (Psalm 46:10). Lamentations tells us, "The Lord is good to those who depend upon Him, to those who search for Him. So it is good to wait quietly for salvation [deliverance] from the Lord" (Lamentations 3:25-26).

Jesus assures us, "Come to Me, all of you who are weary and carry heavy burdens, and I will give you rest … let Me teach you, because I am humble and gentle at heart, and you will find rest for your souls" (Matthew 11:28-29). Don't miss Jesus' request to be our teacher during burdensome times along with His promise of rest. We have much to learn. And, most important, is His call to us during tough times of, "Come to Me"

A.W. Tozer said it best, "God waits to be wanted."[8]

Chapter 1: Questions for Meditation & Discussion

Summary Points for Reflection

1. God's Word, the Bible, is not silent when it comes to the reality of hardships and suffering.

2. Life's hardships are many and we all have them— Christian and non-Christian. The key lies not in the experience, but in our response.

3. It is wrong to believe that God causes and is responsible for every hardship of life.

4. God is well aware of every detail and circumstance of our lives; He is ever-present, engaged, and working even during those times that we may not sense His presence.

5. God is purposeful and can use any experience to accomplish His purpose. Challenging times can reveal and strengthen our areas of weakness, refine our character, grow us in Christlikeness, and prepare us for a new assignment from God.

6. There may be times when we cry for understanding; God's answer may be to trust Him as a loving Father. Trusting God and relying upon Biblical truth even when we don't feel like it is a sure sign of spiritual maturity.

7. God should never be defined through our feelings or circumstances. The truthfulness of God and the Bible is not dependent upon our emotions.

8. Hardships can reveal the true source of our dependence (self, things, or God).

9. Difficult times are unique in that during them we can experience His loving and comforting presence, His faithfulness, and His abundant provision of supernatural joy, hope, and strength.

10. As Christians, like branches to the vine, we are securely attached to Jesus. As we obediently abide in Him, we will experience His peace and produce fruit during times of stress.

11. Match the following key Biblical truths with their listed respective verses:

___ God is not a man and fulfills His promises.

___ God is always with you.

___ God disciplines those He loves.

___ God will never fail or abandon you.

___ God's ways are not man's ways and His thoughts are not man's thoughts.

___ We were created for God's glory.

___ We will experience trials and sorrows.

___ We will experience persecution.

___ Troubles are opportunities.

___ God teaches through suffering.

___ God is with us and holds us up when we stumble and fall.

___ God will restore, strengthen, and support us when we suffer.

___ God hears when we call for help.

___ Problems and trials result in developing Christlike character qualities.

___ We should trust in God and not ourselves or rely on our own insight.

___ Our future is in God's hands.

_____ Don't worry but pray with thankfulness and God
will give you his peace.

_____ Trust in God's unfailing love for you.

_____ Everything God does reveals His glory and all he
does is just and good and trustworthy.

_____ God may allow suffering, but He will lift you up
and restore you.

1.	Isaiah 55:8-9	11.	Psalms 34:17
2.	John 16:33	12.	Romans 5:3-5
3.	2 Timothy 3:12	13.	Isaiah 43:7
4.	Numbers 23:19	14.	Proverbs 3:5
5.	James 1:2	15.	Psalms 31:14-15
6.	Hebrews 12:6	16.	Philippians 4:6-7
7.	Psalms 119:71	17.	Psalms 52:8
8.	Psalms 37:23-24	18.	Hebrews 13:5
9.	1 Peter 5:10	19.	Psalms 16:8
10.	Psalms 71:20-21	20.	Psalms 111:3,7

12. As you look back over your life, think of those times
when you experienced a personal struggle or crisis. What,
if any, impact did these have on your relationship with
God?

13. Examine John 15:1-7. How does a person "abide"? Why is
this important and what can you do to strengthen your
"abiding" in Christ Jesus?

CHAPTER TWO

DOES FAITH MAKE A DIFFERENCE?

If our Christian faith doesn't make a difference in the things that make a difference, then what's the difference? Obviously, adversity certainly falls within the definition of things that make a difference. As Christians, how we view and respond to adversity ought to be different from the world's response. A large part of that difference is our faith that should be based solely upon Biblical truth.

The world's responses are far different than a child of God's. The Apostle Paul rebuked the Corinthian church's worldly behavior when he said, "Aren't you living like people of the world?" (1 Corinthians 3:3). This difference was obvious recently when I had the opportunity to visit a terminally ill and dear Christian friend as he lay in his hospital bed. His doctors had told him the sobering news that all medical means to save him were exhausted. There was nothing more they could do. In effect, they were now making him as comfortable as possible awaiting his death.

Our last conversation was special. The world would expect that he would be filled with panic, fear and tears. To the contrary, as he lay there speaking haltingly with each breath an effort, he was excited. Rather than dwell on his condition, he insisted on telling me what God was doing in the lives of others. He was praising God. What a testimony as he lay in God's waiting room preparing to meet his Lord and Savior! Jesus made a difference.

The world's answers and worldly solutions prove inadequate and are of little comfort in dealing with the pain and loss that often accompany adversity. Human encouragement while sincere falls short. When all seems lost and uncertain, the only thing that dispels our fear and pain, and offers strength, hope, and endurance is our faith that our loving God is a true and trustworthy refuge.

Our faith and reliance upon God's presence and strength to endure life's painful times may not remove the suffering and grief. However, the promise and reality of our eternal destiny that awaits us brings a supernatural peace and acceptance that counters the "sting of death."

A precious mother who recently lost her son described this truth and the role and value of her faith during this heartbreaking loss.

> My story is painful and heartbreaking to tell and relive. It is only by God's grace and the strength He gives that I can express my innermost feelings. One of my two sons had an incurable disease that eventually took his life. As a family, we all suffered as over time we saw the disease taking its toll on his young body. My heart ached and countless days and nights were filled with tears as I dreaded but knew what was inevitably coming. Life goes on and now it is our faith in God that picks up the broken pieces of our hearts and gives us strength to go on and even find meaning when looking back over the past years.
>
> Our Christian faith and belief in God and His promises have always been a foundation in our family. My husband and I gave both of our children

to God even before they were born, and raised them teaching both about God and His beloved Son, Jesus Christ, Who was sent to save us. Our son's physical condition reminded us of the certainty of death and caused us to instruct both children that death was not to be feared. We wanted to make sure they understood the reality and hope of heaven as contained in the Bible. This instruction, however, was not some sterile classroom teaching as we were aware of what the future held for our oldest. It wasn't easy, nor without pain, when the time came for us to personalize our teaching and explain to our youngest son that his brother was not going to get well. We hugged, cried and then through his young tears, he said that his brother would be in heaven with Jesus and would never be sick again and that we all would be together again someday—out of the mouth of our babe, and in the midst of our grief, we were reminded of our heavenly Father's promise.

As a family, we watched our son fight the disease that had invaded his young body. He dealt with the physical pain, and we all suffered seeing one we loved endure such hardship. As time passed and we saw his difficulty and suffering increase, our prayers for improvement and healing changed. We reached the point when we had to surrender our young son to God. We relinquished what we wanted and gave our son to God and His will. As parents, through our tears, we prayed and released our son; it was the hardest prayer that we ever prayed.

In the weeks that followed our son's condition worsened. His last words as he lay in the hospital were his begging for "more, more" of life-giving oxygen—and then he was gone. God had responded by taking him home and answering my son's request for "more." Our "more" would have only prolonged his condition and suffering; God's "more" was to take him to heaven where the Bible tells us in Revelation 21, "God's home is now with His people. God, Himself, will be with them. He will wipe away every tear from their eyes and there will be no more death, sorrow or crying or pain. All these things are gone forever."

Yes, I grieved. My first-born baby had died. My pain was real and the only thing that I held onto was faith in my loving Father who also endured the loss of His only Son, Jesus. My tears still come but over time my sorrow is being replaced with my faith and hope founded on God's promises of where our young son has gone. Our lives are short on this earth, and we have an eternal home in heaven with all our family where there are no diseases, wheelchairs, tears, or hardships—only inexpressible joy and freedom in the presence of our Lord. We know who God is and we know and trust in the truth of His promises. Being in Christ is the safest place in life and in death. In Him alone, we are eternally secure.

One doesn't come out of an experience as this without some changes. For me, it is that my faith is stronger today. God has shown me that I was entirely focused on our son's suffering instead of also seeing the blessings and good God would bring through this experience. Through our son, God taught us to see life more clearly, to appreciate the big and the small, and that God's ways are not ours. So many others have been encouraged and bolstered with God's promises of strength to endure. For our family, the reality of heaven and what awaits us is much more real. With much anticipation I await Christ's return and being reunited with my son. What a joyous time that will be! Until then, we see life much clearer and are thankful for all of the blessings that before we took for granted.

We sometimes become so busy and distracted in everyday life, and particularly in the midst of life's hardships, we forget why we're here. God made us for Himself. Contrary to the world's mantra, it's not about us; it's really all about Jesus. God has a plan for each of us. I am not my own. What a privilege to know and trust Him, be in His presence, and do His will as He leads. God's many blessings, love, and promises far outweigh our circumstances— even the loss of a beloved child. Circumstances will change constantly and many unexpectedly. God never will.

God provided my son with "more" and God's "more" is enough for each of us.

As this mother's testimony reveals, life's crises often produce pain, and various emotions rush to the surface, many which may surprise us. However, such trials afford us a better opportunity to examine and evaluate our concept and beliefs about God. It is easy to conclude that God is good during times of well-being; it is much different to call Him good when all is not well and we are left with no explanations or understanding.

To call God good and maintain a thankful and worshipful spirit in such tenuous times requires a strong faith and clear understanding of God's character. This doesn't come easily or quickly. There is no shortcut; spiritual maturity is the fruit of a lifetime of exercising spiritual disciplines. Primary is regular time alone with God in prayer and allowing Him to reveal Himself in His word, the Bible.

John Piper addressed the decision to either choose the world's agenda or to seek God. "Every moment in every circumstance we stand on the brink between the lure of idolatry and the delight of seeing and knowing God."[9] Our Father God calls us to Himself for comfort, strength, encouragement, hope, and for His good purposes. All the while, the pain is real and those voices inside us and in our culture shout at us to condemn and ignore God and fall victim to the world's responses and counterfeit solutions. The choices are clear. As Job's own wife told him in the midst of his suffering, "Are you still trying to maintain your integrity? Curse God and die!" (Job 2:9). Job chose otherwise and discovered God in unimaginable and glorious ways.

God spoke in Jeremiah 9:23-24 exhorting us, "Don't let the wise boast in their wisdom or the powerful boast in their power, or the rich boast in their riches. But those who wish to boast should boast in this alone, that they truly know Me and understand that I am the Lord."

The world focuses on human wisdom, power, health and riches. This is typically the default for many who respond to pain in worldly fashion. During times of adversity, questions and answers are sought from human wisdom. Depending upon the nature of the hardship, power is exerted or money is used to change the outcome. In contrast, God wants us to focus in seeking and trusting in Him. As Hebrews 11:1 reminds us, "Faith is the confidence that what we hope for will actually happen; it gives us assurance about things we cannot see." Our faith in God is built upon the unseen, the knowledge of who God is and what he is like. The more we seek and grow in knowing God, the more we are able to exercise Biblical wisdom and view life's hardships with faith and a different view than the world.

The object of our faith and trust is in God versus the world;

the unseen versus what we see around us. God gives us assurance through His many promises in the Bible. Circumstances, however, can impact our trusting God during times of adversity and personal pain. With this in mind, Jesus makes a revealing statement in John 7:16-17, "So Jesus answered them and said, 'My teaching is not Mine, but His who sent Me. If anyone is willing to do His will, he will know of the teaching, whether it is of God or whether I speak from Myself.'"

Jesus is telling us to *first* exercise trust in God and *then* discover the truthfulness of God's promises by our obedience. This strikes at the heart of faith and is the opposite of what we naturally crave. We want to "know first" and then decide if we'll "do." Jesus says to "do first" and then you will "know." Faith is not to be the final resort we turn to after all other resources have been exhausted. God is not in the business of providing detailed explanations for curiosity seekers or responding to a "request for a proposal" to then decide if we will trust Him.

In 1887, hymn writer John Sammis well understood Jesus' teachings when he wrote the familiar words we sing today:

When we walk with the Lord in the light of His Word,
What a glory He sheds on our way!
While we do His good will, He abides with us still,
And with all who will trust and obey.

Not a shadow can rise, not a cloud in the skies,
But His smile quickly drives it away;
Not a doubt or a fear, not a sigh or a tear,
Can abide while we trust and obey.

Not a burden we bear, not a sorrow we share,
But our toil He doth richly repay;
Not a grief or a loss, not a frown or a cross,
But is blessed if we trust and obey.

Trust and obey, for there's no other way

To be happy in Jesus, but to trust and obey.[10]

The ability to grow in our faith and stepping out in obedience increases as we grow in our knowing God and His Word. Learning about God and growing in our knowledge of Him is a worthwhile journey. A.W. Tozer writes,

> The Apostle Paul writes of his burning desire to know Christ (Philippians 3:8). 'That I may know Him,' was the goal of his heart and to this end he sacrificed everything … how tragic that we in this dark day have had our seeking done for us by our teachers. Everything is made to center upon the initial act of 'accepting' Christ (a term, incidentally, not found in the Bible) and we are not expected thereafter to crave any further revelation of God to our souls. We have been snared in the coils of a spurious logic which insists that if we have found Him, we need no more seek Him. In the midst of this great chill there are some, I rejoice to acknowledge, who will not be content with shallow logic. They will … hunt for some lonely place and pray, 'O God show me Thy glory.' They want to taste, to touch with their hearts, to see with their inner eyes the wonder of God. Complacency is a deadly foe of all spiritual growth. Right now we are in an age of religious complexity. The simplicity of Christ is rarely found among us. In its place are programs, methods, organizations and a world of nervous activities which occupy time and attention but can never satisfy the longing of the heart. God waits to be wanted.[11]

While it is true that as Christians in our finite knowledge we will never completely know God until we are glorified with

Him in our eternal state, we can grow in our understanding as He reveals himself in the Scriptures. This lifelong growth process develops a foundation that can withstand life's most trying moments in a godly fashion. For those whose lives are characterized by such a foundation, they display an entirely different response to adversity and crisis.

Dr. Richard Blackaby, author, former pastor, and seminary president, provides insight into having a godly perspective during times of hardship.

> In Psalm 11 we see David asking, "If the foundations are destroyed, what can the righteous do?" David wondered this at a time when his enemies were aggressively pursuing his downfall and his friends were urging him to flee. It appeared as if he could lose everything. Yet David chose to evaluate his situation from this starting point: "In the Lord I put my trust." Every decision he made concerning his future was based on his unwavering trust in God. David understood that God allows difficult times. For the wicked, these trials are forms of divine judgment but for the righteous they are times of testing. David passed the test! He concluded: "For the Lord is righteous, He loves righteousness; His countenance beholds the upright." David began his psalm by contemplating running from his problems and trying to save himself. He ended by basking in God's presence. David's hope was not that all he had lost would be restored, or that circumstances would return to the way they once were, or that he would prosper through his adversity. David's thoughts rose higher. He realized that God's presence was all he needed. For David, God was enough. Some Christians want

> God plus success, or wealth, or victory, or . . . David
> found such joy, satisfaction and peace in the divine
> presence, everything else became secondary.[12]

The book of James states an important yet often overlooked truth. "When troubles come your way, consider it an opportunity for great joy. For you know that when your faith is tested, your endurance has a chance to grow. So let it grow, for when your endurance is fully developed, you will be perfect and complete, needing nothing" (James 1:2-4).

Our lives as Christians are subject to hardships and possible crisis that may include painful suffering. Many grumble and some sarcastically joke about "counting it all joy" during these difficult times. This mocks the important teaching in this verse. We are given a promise of the power of endurance. The basis of our "joy" comes from our trust that God will come alongside of us in each difficult time thus giving us the strength to endure. In faith we respond with joy and in doing so, He will use the experience to grow our faith and ability to endure and face more challenging times.

Our faithful endurance brings honor to God and may be used as a witness to others about God's sufficient provision. We may be tempted during hardships to complain and react like the world. However, we are assured in 1 Corinthians 10:12-13, "And God is faithful. He will not allow the temptation to be more than you can stand. When you are tempted, He will show you a way out so that you can endure." No doubt, there are times when God provides deliverance, but we should not miss seeing each difficult situation as a means to grow our endurance. The Apostle Paul modeled this mindset and revealed his strong faith by stating that he was glad to boast and even find pleasure in his weaknesses. He made a bold paradoxical statement that further emphasizes the joy that comes from endurance: "For when I am weak, then I am strong" (2 Corinthians 13:9-10). Such a statement only makes sense when understanding the benefits of a strong and growing faith in God's provision for enduring.

What then is the key to "becoming perfect and complete, needing nothing?" James gives us the answer: Endurance. When viewed from this perspective, we can say that troubles and hardships can serve a positive purpose. They help us reach a mindset that needs nothing but faith in our great God. As said earlier by the mother who lost her young son, "God is enough."

Sally Breedlove asks a very revealing question in her book *Choosing Rest.* "What do you expect life to be?" She discusses the serious implications of how one responds.

> Do you expect your life to be a place where all prayers are answered immediately? A place where we know well in advance that we will have all the resources we need to meet every challenge? A place where none of the scary possibilities that wound and destroy other people will ever happen to us? We long for that first Garden of Eden, but a life of endless ease is a cheap substitute.

> So, what is the "good life"? Paul said, "It is through faith that a righteous person has life" (Galatians 3:11). The implication of this goes far beyond our salvation. We learn that faith is the firm conviction and reality that what we see around us is lacking, and what we currently see and possess do not represent the future glory that one day will be ours.

> To live by faith means that invisible spiritual realities and promises about the future will give our hearts strength. It means we acknowledge that blessings and assurances in this present world are not the gate to true heart rest. Our fears rarely have

present-tense answers—that's why the choice to live by faith is the only way out of the stronghold of worry. If we want more than an existence where we attempt to protect ourselves and those we love, the only recourse we have is faith—the choice to trust the goodness of God in the face of a very imperfect and incomplete reality.[13]

David provides a worthwhile example for us and gives us assurance of God's readiness to respond to our need for strength and hope. First Samuel 30:1-20 describes one of the low points in David's life. David and his men had returned to their village to discover their enemy had raided, burned, and crushed their homes. Women and children were carried away. All of David's men were grieving, hurt and bitter about losing their homes and families. They "wept until they would weep no more." Their grief turned to anger and they focused blame on David. Anger quickly produced vengeance as they talked about stoning David for leading them away from their homes. In addition to suffering great personal loss, David was in great danger.

While our experience will differ from David's, the emotions that arise during times of adversity may be similar, if not the same, i.e., loss, grief, abandonment, danger, fear, disappointment in friends, and uncertainty. From the world's view, David's life was spinning out of control. However, in the midst of tragedy and hopelessness, and contrary to man's perspective, a simple phrase in 1 Samuel 30:6 serves as a guide during such times, "But David found strength in the Lord his God." Scripture then reveals, "David brought everything back" (1 Samuel 30:19). God is a God of restoration. He may not bring everything back as with David; but He can restore us by His strength to endure regardless of the situation.

Even when we grieve and cry out to Him seeking under-standing and strength to just get through the long days of pain and suffering, we can be assured that God is engaged; He hears; He loves; He responds; we are His beloved. There is hope; God is in control.

Be comforted by our loving God's promise.

> *He (God) Himself has said, I will not in any way fail you nor give you up, nor leave you without support. I will not, I will not, I will not in any degree leave you helpless, nor forsake, nor let you down, or relax my hold on you. So we take comfort and are encouraged and confidently and boldly say, The Lord is my helper, I will not fear or dread or be terrified, what can man do to me?*
>
> —HEBREWS 13:5-6 AMPLIFIED BIBLE

Chapter 2: Does Faith Make A Difference?

Summary Points for Reflection

1. As Christians, how we view and respond to adversity ought to be radically different from the world's response.

2. The world's answers and solutions to hardship prove inadequate and provide little comfort or meaning for the pain that often accompanies adversity.

3. It is easy to call God good and be thankful during times of well-being; it's quite another during times of suffering and pain.

4. God calls us to Himself for comfort, strength, encouragement, and hope. Like the Good Shepherd that He is, He cares for His wounded sheep.

5. A growing faith and knowledge of God lays a strong foundation to withstand life's trials while trusting that He is aware, engaged, and will never leave or forsake us. Never.

6. God wants us to focus and grow in knowing Him. This is a lifelong process requiring discipline of spending regular time with Him as He reveals Himself through His Word, the Bible.

7. Our faith is built upon the unseen and Biblical truth of God. The more we know God the more we are able to view life's hardships differently from the world and draw upon His abundant resources.

8. The fruit of a growing strong faith is endurance through difficult times. God is enough.

9. God's Word assures us that He is our helper and we need not be afraid or terrified. We are His beloved and we can trust in Him. He is in control.

Chapter 2: Questions for Meditation & Discussion

1. What is the Scriptural truth contained in the following verses:

   Hebrews 13:5, Matthew 6:8, 1 John 3:20

2. How does Hebrews 11:1 describe "faith" and what is the basis of "confidence" and "assurance"?

3. In Philippians 3:8, the Apostle Paul describes his passion and longing to grow in "knowing Christ". What do you believe he means by wanting to grow in "knowing Christ"?

4. What things must you do in order to really know someone? When you truly know someone, list all the possible things about that person that you will know. How does this apply to your relationship with God?

5. Recognizing that life is filled with various forms of adversity and challenges, what can you do to prepare and increase your faith?

CHAPTER THREE

I THOUGHT GOD LOVED ME!

At our house, Saturdays are special. They bring several young Christian men to our home before sunrise for Bible study. During one of these times, I posed a few questions to the group, many of whom who are going through some tough times.

What is the relationship between God's love and times of hardship?

Does God have a mission for you personally, and, if so, what is it and how does it relate to times when you experience hardship?

My questions were greeted with a variety of responses. When talking about God's love, all readily acknowledged His love but were honest in admitting the difficulty of making the connection of this truth to times of hardship. Although unspoken, God's love was implicitly suspect or conditional.

The personal mission question generated several answers. They all were good and had a Biblical source; however, I noticed two key elements missing: a clear statement defining God's mission for each of us and its relevance during times of adversity.

Having a Biblical perspective on hardships that test us and brings suffering to our life must start with an understanding of two equally important truths: God's love and God's mission. It's vital to understand the connection between these two and the reality of life's painful events. Hardships must be framed within the context of these truths.

God's incredible love for us, His children, provides the basis for a trusting faith. God's mission provides a cause and purpose that gives meaning and direction to our lives especially during times of personal crisis. Understanding both His love and His mission for us gives perspective and insight into His will and plan for our lives. They both are inextricably connected.

God's Incredible Love

As Christians, we hear and speak of God's love for His children. Jeremiah 31:3 describes His love, "I [God] have loved you, my people with an everlasting love. With unfailing love I have drawn you to myself." How many times have we heard and recited John 3:16, "For God so loved the world that He gave His one and only Son"? Our familiarity may result in taking such an expression of love for granted. We may acknowledge this truth intellectually, but fail to consider the full implications of this profound truth and what it says about God.

Dr. James Dobson underscored this wonderful truth in his book, *When God Doesn't Make Sense*, "One of the most breathtaking concepts in all of Scripture is the revelation that God knows each of us personally and that we are in His mind both day and night. There is no way to comprehend the full implications of this love by the King of kings and Lord of lords."[14]

Growth in our relationship with God comes with understanding, accepting, experiencing, and learning to trust and rest confidently in God's love. This truth is critical if we are to understand and find purpose and comfort during times of hardship.

God's presence and provision during times of difficulty reflect His love and caring. Jesus taught His followers in Matthew 7:9-11 about His loving Father when He said, "So, if you sinful people know how to give good gifts to your children, how much more will your heavenly Father give good gifts to those who ask him." Admittedly, God's good gifts may be different from the quick deliverance we often request when our life becomes difficult. His greatest gift may be one of endurance.

No doubt, God can do or allow anything He wishes. And, there will be times when He does provide deliverance and answers our heart's desires. However, it may be that the better gifts are the lessons learned during trials and the resulting strengthening of our faith.

As our loving Father, His love always translates to His providing the resources needed to endure life's challenges. God's gifts may take the shape of His sustaining grace that enables endurance with an unexplainable and supernatural peace.

God's Mission

To illustrate the importance of mission, allow me to use a personal business analogy.

For a number of years in my role as head of a large corporation, it was important that every employee know and understand our business mission. This gave focus and direction. It allowed the development of criteria as to what we should or shouldn't be doing. Once the mission was clear, then priorities, projects, and actions fell into line. Everything we did or considered doing was evaluated in terms of helping us accomplish our mission. Likewise, we passed up many good initiatives if they didn't contribute to the mission.

But being committed to a mission has a difficult side. Unpopular or painful adjustments were often necessary to keep the business on track. To protect the integrity and commitment to the mission, we often faced gut-wrenching decisions that included job eliminations, reorganizations, and employee replacement. The pursuit of the mission included pain.

Is there a spiritual application? Does God have a mission and purpose for us as His children?

The answer is a simple "Yes." God has always had a mission. The problem is that we often fail to identify His mission or to consider its relevance to our lives. Would God allow us to go through a painful situation if His divine mission was advanced or if we were strengthened and prepared to play a greater role in accomplishing that mission? I would hope you would agree and answer, "Yes."

Would God allow us to experience a painful situation in order to advance His mission? Would He use hardship to prepare us to play a greater role in accomplishing that mission? We need look no farther than God's only Son, Jesus, to answer these questions. God allowed Him to suffer pain, rejection and humiliation, all culminating in the horrific public death by crucifixion to finish the work and God's mission for His life which was to take upon Himself the just penalty for our sins and thus providing us a Savior. In Jesus' final prayer as recorded in John 17:4, He said to His Father God, "I brought glory to you here on earth by completing the work you gave me to do." And, in John 19:30 Jesus refers to His completion of His Father's work and mission as He said, "It is finished."

Undoubtedly, the work included by Jesus accomplishing His mission will differ greatly from ours. Also, it would be a mistake to assume that we will have the same degree of faith and intimacy as He had with His Father God. However the lesson is that like Jesus each of us is called to honor and bring glory to God in every experience of life—in good or bad times. This is our mission.

The Apostle Paul in his letter to the Ephesians states, "He (God) has created us anew in Christ Jesus, so we can do the good things he planned for us long ago." (Ephesians 2:10b) The good things that God desires always results in Him being honored and glorified. And, as quoted earlier, Isaiah 43:7 speaks of God's purpose for us, "Bring all who claim me as their God, for I have made them for my glory. It was I who created them." We were created to bring glory to God.

God's glory is a prominent theme throughout the Bible and hasn't changed. "Glory to God" is mentioned seventy-eight times. If you add all references to glory, glorify, honor, and honoring God, the number exceeds three thousand times in the Bible. His message to the world has been and is today to show himself as the Lord, there is no other.

Jesus underscores the importance of glorifying and honoring God when He said, "Let your light shine before men in such a way that they may see your good works, and glorify your Father who is in heaven" (Matthew 5:16 NAS). The Apostle Paul reminded the Corinthians that "Whatever you do, do it all for the glory of God" (1 Corinthians 10:31).

Christian history testifies to the importance of our living for God's glory. One of the key beliefs driving the Protestant Reformation was *Soli Deo Gloria*, a Latin term for "Glory to God alone." This underscored that everything done is for God's glory to the exclusion of man's self-glorification and pride. Christians are to be motivated and inspired by God's glory versus their own.

God spoke through His servant Isaiah, "I am the Lord; there is no other God. I have equipped you for battle, though you don't even know Me, so all the world from east to west will know there is no other God. I am the Lord, and there is no other. I create the light and make the darkness. I send good times and bad times. I, the Lord, am the One who does these things" (Isaiah 45:5-7). He assures us that He equips us for battle in good and bad times to show that He is God to bring honor and glory to Himself. Life's adversities and hardships fall in the category of the "battle of bad times."

As mentioned earlier, I find it interesting when asking Christians the question, "What is God's mission for you?" that some quote Jesus' Great Commission as given in Matthew 28:19-20 of going and making disciples. Undoubtedly, this is a vital component of every Christian's mission. What better way to glorify and bring honor to God than to be actively involved in introducing others to our Savior Jesus?

Recognizing the consistent emphasis throughout the Bible upon bringing glory to God along with the Great Commission, we can say that God's mission for every Christian is

> *To love, honor, and glorify God*
> *and be an active participant in fulfilling*
> *His Great Commission.*

If we are to give glory to God during life's trials and adversities by enduring, then we must trust that He will provide enabling grace and strength. We are assured that God will in 2 Peter 1:3, "By His divine power, God has given us everything we need for living a godly life." No doubt, living in a godly manner includes those challenging times of hardship. Enduring and reacting "godly" when experiencing adversity must come from God and His power and not self-effort. We can't rise above many of life's extreme crises on our own. This dramatically differs from the world's resources or answers for coping.

Life's trials present opportunities to fulfill His mission by our reaction and behavior. God is trustworthy and will provide His supernatural strength for enduring while understanding that, although painful, many hardships are related to serving His purpose. The real question is not will He sustain us, but rather will we submit to and seek Him? He is engaged and fully aware of what's happening. Recognizing this, the right response is not, "Why?" but rather, "How can I bring honor to God in the midst of this painful situation?"

It's important at this point to emphasize again that it is wrong to assume that God is responsible or causes all hardships. What is important is to understand that regardless of the origin or type of hardship, God can use it for His good purpose. Sources of adversity and purpose in trials are discussed at some length in a following chapter.

The world's trite answers "to hang on and be strong" are quite different and fall short in finding purpose or providing meaningful solutions to withstand life's trials. This difference was made evident to me early in my business career when I attended a conference conducted by a secular humanistic organization. The focus of the training was how to deal with employees' personal problems in a business environment. Unfortunately, the solutions and techniques touted were severely lacking and anything but godly.

At the conclusion of the conference that focused entirely on the potential problems and negative scenarios that might occur, the trainer had the group form a large circle and hold hands. Then he closed the training by pronouncing, "Life is hell and is full of problems and crisis. We must be strong." He next held up everyone's hands clasped together and pronounced, "All we've got to cope and survive is one another!" How tragic and devoid of purpose and the good news of our hope and resources in Christ! Needless to say, the participants were far from encouraged and left with a fragile and hopeless survivor mentality.

Our Role in God's Mission

Accomplishing God's mission will differ individually. Our roles will vary. For some it may be the more visible front lines; for others it may be a behind-the-scenes role of serving. Every job or task regardless of how menial it may appear is divine in nature and should play a role in God's mission. The expectation is that wherever we are and whatever we're doing, and in whatever circumstance we find ourselves, we are to bring honor and glory to him. Likewise, we must always be sensitive to being a positive witness and playing a role in the fulfilling of Jesus' Great Commission which brings high honor to our Father God.

For many years, I had the misleading belief that those who were serious about God should go into full-time ministry. While it is true that many are called in this direction, it fostered the prevalent concept of dualism that exists today between pastors and the laity. I mistakenly separated God from my day-to-day world. My faith and Christianity were neatly compartmentalized and conveniently acted out when I was in church. I played an assortment of roles suitable to where I was whether in church, with family, in the workplace, or in social arenas.

This thinking demeaned the important mission of lay people involved in the ministry of serving God and his mission wherever they are in the world. Ephesians 4:12 is clear that all God's children are to be equipped to do His work (God's mission). This command applies to each of us. Since the majority of us are in the workplace or in the home, then we should be mission-minded and view our work and family environment as divine assignments from God. Thus marriages, parenting, jobs, careers, social involvement—all should reflect God and bring honor to him.

The Apostle Paul further affirmed God's mission in his admonition in 2 Corinthians 5:19-20 by telling us that God was in Christ, reconciling the world to himself, and that he now has given us this wonderful message of reconciliation—so we are ambassadors for Christ through which God makes his appeal to the world! And, later in 1 Corinthians 15:58, Paul closes his message to the Corinthians by telling them to "...be strong and immovable. Always work enthusiastically for the Lord." We shouldn't interpret this admonition to be directed to pastoral staff alone.

We, as Christians, have an assignment, a mission, and work to do wherever God has placed us. John R.W. Stott speaks of our commission as Christians in his book, *Basic Christianity*, "The Christian life is a family affair, in which the children enjoy fellowship with their Father and with each other. But let it not for one moment be thought that this exhausts the Christian's responsibilities. Christians are not a self-regarding coterie of smugs and selfish prigs, who are interested only in themselves. On the contrary, every Christian should be deeply concerned about all his fellow men. Although every Christian is not called to be a minister or a missionary, God does intend every Christian to be a witness to Jesus Christ. In his home, among friends, at college, at his place of business, it is his solemn responsibility to live a consistent, loving, humble, honest, Christ-like life, and to seek to win other people for him. He will be discreet and courteous, but determined." [15]

Paul exhorts us throughout Scripture to grow and walk in a manner consistent with what we have received in Christ Jesus. In Galatians 2:20 he gives us a vivid description of the life we should be living and displaying to the world when he says, "I have been crucified with Christ; and it is no longer I who live, but Christ lives in me; and the life which I now live in the flesh I live by faith in the Son of God, who loved me and gave Himself up for me" (NASB). As God's children, we should carry forward God's mission of bringing glory to Him and helping advance his Kingdom by letting Christ live in us.

Paul exhorted the Philippians to "Work hard to show the results of your salvation, obeying God with deep reverence and fear. For God is working in you, giving you the desire and power to do what pleases Him" (Philippians 2:12-13). What is it that pleases God? Is it not participating in his mission and bringing Him honor, glory and helping populate His kingdom?

A few years ago, it was my privilege to participate with a small group of other corporate Christian CEOs called upon to identify the primary challenges experienced upon retirement. The discussion was revealing. The group identified two major problems: the loss of personal identity and the absence of any purpose for life. Keep in mind that this was a group of dedicated Christians. I was surprised, but understood.

One of the subtle mindsets developed over a lifetime of working is exchanging one's personal identity for business identity or job title. In essence, what you do becomes who you are, your identity. It's how you identify yourself. Typically the first thing we ask someone upon meeting them is, "What do you do?" This reinforces and places one's personal identity in the hands of the workplace. Retirement or losing a job then is not just being out of work, it is a much deeper emotional loss; it's losing one's personal identity. For me, I was the chairman, CEO, and president, and upon retiring, this identity was gone.

In similar fashion, many business leaders are prone to take for themselves their respective company's mission as their own life mission. Years are spent building a business or achieving career goals. When this ends, mission and purpose are left behind. The most common statement heard by such professionals is, "My days are too long; I don't know what to do or where to go." Is it any wonder why job losses or retirements (aside from the financial impact) can have such a devastating impact! Misplaced personal identity and sense of purpose are gone.

A close friend and former corporate officer told me that upon retirement he commenced to complete his "to do" list around his home. Upon completion, he said he went inside, sat down, and told his wife that all was done and he was now ready to die. How sad.

Before the group of CEOs dismissed, time was devoted to discussing the error and deceit found in these two problems. As Christians, our identity is in Christ and not in any job, position, or title. We never lose that identity and personal relationship we have as Christians with our Lord and Savior Jesus. The Apostle Paul underscored our identity in Christ when he said, "it is no longer I who live, but Christ lives in me" (Galatians 2:20).

Second, our mission is from God, not a business. It makes no difference if one is a janitor or CEO, identity and mission do not change with job loss, change, or retirement. The arena or audience may change, but our identity in Christ and working to accomplish God's mission is unchanged. Businesses and job titles are fleeting and a means and not an end. God has placed each of us right where He desires with an assignment to work and perform in a manner that brings Him honor and glory, which is His mission.

When I retired and was no longer the head of a large corporation, my identity in Christ didn't change nor did my personal mission of seeking out new ways to honor and glorify Christ. My arena changed and the means to accomplish God's mission changed, but my identity and mission remained intact.

God has commissioned us as ambassadors for Christ (2 Corinthians 5:20) with an assigned mission in this world. He desires that each of His children grow in spiritual maturity and be equipped for His use and purpose. Understanding this, God will use various means to draw us to Himself and make us more effective. Tough times may be used to strengthen our faith and better prepare us for His assignments wherever He places us.

We also must understand that God's ways and thoughts are far different than ours (Isaiah 55:8). There may be times when His means of accomplishing His mission are far different than what we like. Some may include what the world would consider a crisis; some may not be understood. We can only rest in God's love, trust Him, and recognize that He is engaged and purposeful. The experience may have a primary role in his mission.

The knowledge of God's love and mission are paramount to understanding many of life's troubles. Without this, tragedies make little sense!

Chapter 3: I Thought God Loved Me!

Summary Points for Reflection

1. God's love provides the basis for a trusting faith and a growing loving relationship with Him as we become more like Christ.

2. God's mission provides a cause and purpose that gives meaning and direction especially during times of personal crisis.

3. God's mission is for every believer to love, honor, and glorify God and be an active participant in fulfilling His Great Commission. The expectation is that wherever we are, whatever we're doing, and in whatever circumstance we find ourselves, we are to bring honor and glory to Him.

4. One of the most revolutionary truths in all of Scripture is that God knows each of us personally and is aware and engaged in and around us.

5. Growth comes with understanding and learning to trust and rest confidently in God's love and His promises. This is critical if we are to understand and find purpose and comfort during times of hardship.

6. God can provide deliverance from any hardship. However, the better gift is the spiritual growth resulting from endurance and the positive witnessing impact.

7. Many of life's trials are related to God's purpose and present the opportunity to fulfill His mission by our response. The right question during such times is not, "Why?", rather, "How can this bring honor to God?"

8. Endurance is not based on self-effort; God has promised everything needed to go through each of life's hardships in a God-honoring manner.

9. We should be mission-minded and view our work and

family environment as divine assignments from God. Thus marriage, parenting, jobs, careers, social involvement—all should reflect God and bring honor to Him.

10. God will use various means to draw us to Himself and to make us more effective as we work to accomplish His purpose and mission. Tough times may be used to strengthen our faith and prepare us for new and greater assignments as His ambassadors.

Chapter 3: Questions for Meditation & Discussion

1. What is the truth stated in Jeremiah 31:3?

2. What is the promise Jesus gave in Matthew 7:9-11?

3. What is said about "work" in the following verses?

> John 17:4
> Ephesians 2:10b
> Ephesians 4:12
> Matthew 28:19-20
> 2 Timothy 3:16-17

4. In 2 Corinthians 5:19-20, the Apostle Paul exhorts us as Christians to be "ambassadors for Christ." What is the definition of an "ambassador" and how does this spiritually apply to your life?

5. What do these verses reveal about the enabling source of power available for God's children?

> Philippians 2:12-13
> 1 Corinthians 2:4
> Colossians 1:11
> 2 Timothy 1:7
> Ephesians 3:14-19

6. What specifically can you begin to do/act in order to be a participant in God's mission?

CHAPTER FOUR

DOES GOD EVEN CARE?

Sadly, there are those times of hardship and suffering when immediate relief does not come and we believe God ignores our prayers. This may cause us to abandon prayer and question whether God even cares about us.

We shouldn't have to doubt the depth of God's caring and love. Because of His intense and deep love for us, He sent His only Son to death. Scripture assures us that God cares even about a small sparrow bird (Matthew 10:30-31). How much more then does He care about those for whom He sacrificed His own Son?

On the Sea of Galilee, when Jesus and His disciples were caught in a severe storm and faced the likely prospect of drowning, these close followers of Christ reacted in fear, panic and, desperation and shouted to a sleeping Jesus, "Master, Master, we're going to drown!'" (Luke 8:24). Mark's account in 4:38-40 reveals their mistaken feelings, "Teacher, don't you care that we're going to drown!"

It's interesting that Jesus chose to sleep during this time in the boat, especially while His disciples were anxious and plagued with fear. One can only imagine them scrambling, shouting to one another, terrified, bailing water and frantically trying to control the boat with their own strength. When they had exhausted all means of human effort, they finally turned to

Jesus. He rebuked them, "Why are you so afraid? Do you still have no faith?" Then He calmed the storm and sea.

There may be those times in our lives when we feel our boat is sinking, and, like the disciples, react in fear and wondering, "Where is God?" or "Does He even care?" We would do well to consider Jesus' response and His calling into question their lack of faith.

Why was it that when the storm suddenly appeared, the disciples' first response was to solve the problem themselves apart from Jesus. Then, when it became apparent their efforts were going to be unsuccessful, they turned to Him. When life's hardships appear, our immediate response should be to call upon Jesus. We have to confess that deep within each of us is the need to control all of life's situations including challenges and hardships. Our default seems first to try every human means possible, and then, when all else fails, go to God for help. How wrong this is.

God wants to move us from independence to dependence on Him, and Him alone. He may allow the source of our dependence and the objects of our faith that are outside of Him to be tested to prove their inadequacy. It's important that we move from self control to trust, from independence to dependence.

We should note that it was Jesus' idea to cross the sea at night, not the disciples' idea. We can assume that the experienced fishermen, Peter, Andrew, James, and John, were familiar with the risks involved in a night crossing. Adversity may come not because we have done something wrong; instead it may come so that God can teach us and grow our faith in being dependent upon Him. God wants us to learn from these lessons through Scripture so that we don't have to relearn the lesson in our own life.

The disciples were not the only ones who mistakenly accused Jesus of not caring. In John 11, two sisters, Mary and Martha, were anxious and frustrated with Jesus. They sent word to Him that their brother, Lazarus, was near death. We shouldn't forget that these were real people. We can be sure they experienced worry, grief, and even anger as Lazarus's condition worsened. When Jesus arrived too late, they rebuked Him for His delay. The sisters loved their brother and probably tried every means at their disposal to care for him but it was obvious he was slipping away. One or perhaps both of them remembered how Jesus healed the sick. They frantically sent word for Him to come, confident that He would respond quickly to His close friends. Can you visualize one of the sisters sitting at Lazarus's bedside calling out repeatedly, "Is He here yet? Is He here yet?" while the other sister nervously paced, keeping watch out the window for Jesus to appear. He didn't; Lazarus died. John 11:6 tells us that Jesus purposely delayed. His delay even shocked the disciples and they questioned why He lingered and didn't run to the aid of a friend.

Can you imagine the feelings the sisters experienced? When Jesus finally arrived, the sisters verbally attacked him about his delay, "Lord, if only you had been here, my brother would not have died!" (John 11:21). This single verse doesn't capture all the emotion and grief the sisters felt. Implicit was their charge that Jesus didn't care and paid little attention to their need. They knew He healed others and we can only imagine their thoughts: "Why not Lazarus? You helped others; why not us?" Sound familiar?

Yet, even in her anxiety, Martha expressed her faith in Jesus when she added, "But even now I know that God will give You [Jesus] whatever You ask" (John 11:22). Jesus later revealed a far greater purpose for His delay when He called Lazarus out from his tomb. After this miracle which demonstrated His deity and mission, He reminded the sisters, "Didn't I tell you that you would see God's glory if you believe?" (John 11:40).

Developing a "God doesn't care" attitude is irrational and

contrary to Scriptural truth. Such can be self-destructive and produce a hardened heart toward God. This mindset is a lie from Satan, the great deceiver, who takes every opportunity to discredit, misrepresent, and impugn God's very character and attributes.

We would do well to follow the instructions in Hebrews 3:13, "You must warn each other every day, while it is still 'today,' so that none of you will be deceived by sin and hardened against God." We are warned of Satan's tactics in 2 Thessalonians 2:9-10 and his use of "counterfeit power and signs and miracles. He will use every kind of evil deception to fool." If Satan is allowed to convince a child of God that his or her heavenly Father doesn't care then the victory is his. This should never be allowed to happen.

The battle for a Christian's soul is over. God has won. The next best thing that Satan can do is to render that person's witness ineffective and prevent any participation in God's mission and Christ's Great Commission. The adversary will use any means possible to discredit God and reshape God into one that doesn't care. Stay on guard!

Chapter 4: Does God Even Care?

Summary Points for Reflection

1. Scripture assures us repeatedly that God loves us beyond what we will ever imagine. We should never wonder about the depth of God's caring and love.

2. Developing a "God doesn't care" attitude is contrary to Biblical truth and can be self-destructive and produce a hardened heart toward God. This mindset is from Satan.

3. God wants us to move from independence to dependence on Him, and Him alone.

The battle for a Christian's soul is over. God has won.

Chapter 4: Questions for Meditation & Discussion

1. What is the proof that God does, in fact, care deeply for you?

2. First John 4:19 states that we love Him [God] because He first loved us. Explain this verse and what it means that God loved us first? What is the significance of Him first loving us?

3. What truths are revealed in the following verses?

   > Matthew 10:30-31

   > Romans 5:8

   > Romans 8:31-39

   > 1 John 4:7,16-17

4. First John 4:18 states that "perfect love expels all fear". Explain this truth and the relationship between love and fear?

5. Describe the important lessons that Jesus taught in these two incidents:

   > The disciples, John 11:1-45

   > The sisters, Mary and Martha, Luke 10:38-42

6. Write out John 3:16 in your own words.

CHAPTER FIVE

WHERE DOES THIS STUFF COME FROM?

G od is purposeful and wastes no experience.

It is important to understand that God can and often does use our experiences for His purpose in our lives or the world. This doesn't necessarily mean that He causes or orchestrates each and every crisis. In His omniscience, He is never surprised and knows precisely every detail of our lives, but to say He is then responsible for all the bad in the world is simply untrue.

The question then arises: Where does this stuff come from? What are the sources of hardship? And, how might God use adversity and tough times for His good in our lives? With these questions in mind, it's helpful to identify and understand the possible sources of hardship before suggesting Biblically correct responses.

1. There are seven possible sources of hardships.

2. Life's troubles in this fallen world

3. Suffering for Christ

4. Discipline of God

5. Training in godliness

6. The cost of discipleship and following Christ

7. The consequences of bad or foolish decisions and actions

8. The judgment of God

We should be aware of each of these possibilities so that we may more easily discern what is or isn't God's activity. Times of hardship should prompt us to examine our lives. We need to be sensitive to what God may be teaching us or what He may be seeking to accomplish. Also, it is important to understand that even in the worst of hardships and crisis, God can use the results to accomplish His good and purpose.

Life's normal troubles, trials, and consequences of living in a fallen world.

Repeated six times in Genesis 1 is, "And God said it was good" which describes how He felt as He created the world. God's proclamation revealed a world without death, pain, tears, or suffering; there were no disappointments, sickness, or disease; job losses never happened and food and everything needed was readily accessible; persecution did not exist, nor did discrimination. In essence, there were no hardships, no crises! Stop for a minute and consider this amazing Biblical truth. God's original creation was perfect, harmonious, pure, and pleasing for Him. He pronounced it as good.

This certainly is not representative of our world today.

Something happened in Genesis 3 that changed God's good in creation. Man chose to disobey God by yielding to Satan's temptation. Believing Satan's words that he will be like God, man chose to bypass God in deciding what's right or wrong for life. The results are recorded later in Genesis 3, "All your life you will struggle." Soon after this we see the appearance of pain, jealousy, murder, and death! Where did hardships causing pain and suffering originate? Man's own choice.

There are those who mistakenly conclude that since God created everything, then it follows that God created evil. St.

Augustine correctly reasoned that evil, adversity, suffering, and pain are the result of the absence of God in much the same way that blindness is the absence of sight, darkness is the absence of light, disease is the absence of health, hatred and murder are the absence of love, etc. Therefore he surmises that God did not create evil; *evil is the absence of God.* Genesis 3 describes the results of man choosing to live apart from and absent of God.

God is good and all of God's original creation was good. By man's choice, evil and all other negative consequences were born. This was not part of God's original design or creation. James 1:13-17 touches on this truth, "And, remember, when you are being tempted, do not say, 'God is tempting me.' God is never tempted to do wrong and he never tempts anyone else. Temptation comes from our own desires that entice us and drag us away. These desires give birth to sinful actions. And when sin is allowed to grow, it gives birth to death. So don't be misled... whatever is good and perfect comes down to us from God our Father."

Every disaster and tragedy can be traced to the fact that sin entered the world first through Satan's rebellion and then with the temptation and yielding of Adam and Eve. The Bible confirms, "When Adam sinned, sin entered the world. Adam's sin brought death, so death spread to everyone, for everyone sinned" (Romans 5:12). Man's sin resulted in a curse upon all creation that carries forward today. God's original creation was perfection; man by his own choice introduced imperfection and separation from God resulting in evil, harmful, and painful consequences.

Evil people do evil things and there are times when good people, many of whom are Christians, are hurt, suffer, or even killed. Living in a fallen world carries with it the consequences of adversities as the following Scriptures address:

when troubles come your way; consider it an opportunity for great joy. For you know that when your faith is tested, your endurance has a chance to grow. —JAMES 1:2-4

Note that this Scripture says "when" and not "if" troubles come your way.

Here on earth you will have many trials and sorrows. —JOHN 16:33

God sends rain on the just and unjust alike. —MATTHEW 5:45

When you work in a quarry, stones might fall and crush you! When you chop wood, there is danger with each stroke of your ax! —ECCLESIASTES 10:9

How frail is humanity! How short is life, how full of trouble! —JOB 14:1

Contrary to the Scriptural truths noted above is the popular but errant theology that "itches peoples ears" (2 Timothy 4:3 NLT) and caters to the desire for a life of ease free from problems. This "name it-claim it" or "health and wealth prosperity gospel" is a distortion of Scripture that redefines God's purpose and Christianity to fit man's desires for comfort and perpetual self-centered pleasure.

How sad is the brand of Christianity that omits any expectation or mention of suffering for Christ or experiences of hardship. The errant view that God delivers health, prosperity, and success, and thus brings honor to himself is contrary to the teaching of the Bible and is one of Satan's many lies. False teachers abound marketing Christianity as pain-free and a panacea for eliminating all problems and hardships of life or some guarantee for material success. When their followers experience life's trials (as they surely will) their faith is questioned. Unfortunately, many of these suffering believers are then relegated to second-class status without sufficient faith entitling them to earn lives free from hardships and enjoyment of financial success. What heresy!

Dr. Ed Murphy refutes such teaching in his *Handbook for Spiritual Warfare*, "Suffering is normative for believers. Suffering is part of the believers' identification with Christ. It is no isolated theme; it permeates the Bible. Nowhere is this clearer than in 1 Peter 2:21, 'To this you were called, because Christ suffered for you, leaving you an example that you should follow in His steps.' Suffering, even persecution, follows as a result of this imitation of Christ. Normal Christianity, then, includes suffering."[16]

It is also incorrect and contrary to the Bible to say that all problems are caused by spiritual immaturity just as it is to say that exposure to Biblical teaching will remove all hardships and suffering. The Apostle Paul would be considered lacking in faith at best or, at worst, a failure if such false criteria were applied to his life with his many beatings, imprisonments, and hardships. All of our Lord's apostles except two (John and Judas) experienced a martyr's death and thus would fail this unscriptural test; and our Lord Jesus whose life ended in suffering and death after even his own disciples deserted him would fail using such false teaching. Again, heresy!

Our desire for personal comfort, material gain, and success coupled with this false doctrine produces an unbiblical and catastrophic misguided expectation. Jesus rebuked the Pharisees in Matthew 15:9, "Their worship is a farce for they teach man-made ideas as commands from God." The present-day false teachers who preach man-made health and wealth Christianity fall under this same condemnation.

Life itself contradicts such false beliefs as lives are filled with painful experiences. People get sick, people die, accidents occur, businesses fail, crimes happen, people lose jobs, natural disasters occur, and many other negative and often painful events can lay claim to our desired, peace-filled lives. James 1:2 reads, "*When* troubles come" not *if* they come!

Jesus taught in Matthew 5:45 that the "rain falls on the just and unjust alike." Christians don't have a supernatural umbrella that shields them and keeps them immune from hardships and possible suffering. Living in a "fallen world" subjects Christians and non-Christians to the resulting adversities and often painful effects of sin. Our natural tendency as Christians is to expect avoidance or deliverance from such experiences. No doubt, God can and may prevent things from happening or answer our prayer requests; however, Scripture and life itself tell us this is not always so.

Consider Isaiah 57:1-2, "Good people pass away; the godly often die before their time. But no one seems to care or wonder why. No one seems to understand that God is protecting them from the evil to come. For those who follow godly paths will rest in peace when they die." Like the words in the warranty of a small appliance, "The manufacturer reserves the right to repair or replace at its option."

Often through the eyes of grief and pain, God gives the grace and faith to see as He sees. We can trust Him and know that what God chooses is always best. Sometimes God chooses to replace our damaged and fallen body and mind with one that will never suffer pain or tears, or be tired, or discouraged, or sad, or bored, or too cold or hot under the summer sun. There may be times when we may think God hasn't answered our prayers or that He was uncaring and cruel. However, such thoughts are inconsistent with His character and His attributes—and, in particular, His love that far exceeds our own.

We may not understand why a loved one or a child was taken

from us and question the good that possibly could come from such a heart-breaking event. At such times, our focus needs to be directed upon our loving and almighty Father God and also the place where our Christian loved ones have gone, a far better place than where we are now and one where we will go and join them in our eternal home.

We can learn from David's experience in the loss of his child in 2 Samuel 12:15-23. While the baby was critically sick and near death, David "begged God to spare the child. He went without food and lay all night on the bare ground. The elders of his household pleaded with him to get up and eat with them, but he refused. Then, on the seventh day, the child died...David... realized what had happened and got up from the ground...went into the Tabernacle and worshiped the Lord." When questioned as to why he was not grief stricken when he learned of the child's death? He replied, "I fasted and wept while the child was alive and believed that perhaps the Lord will be gracious to me and let the child live. But why should I fast when he is dead? Can I bring him back again? I will go to be with him one day, but he cannot return to me.' Then David comforted his wife."

David poured out his requests to God to save the child. He went to extremes in his pleading with God in making his prayers known. However, David recognized that God is God and knows better than us regarding what is best and good, even when we may not readily understand. David trusted in God and was well aware of the promise of eternity and his being reunited with the child in God's heaven.

We must understand that as we live in a fallen world, we are subject to this world's negative circumstances and consequences. We should not feel guilty when experiencing heartfelt grief and suffering; pain and loss hurts, and having faith and trust in God doesn't prevent natural tears and sorrow that may accompany some of life's events, nor should it. However, our faith and hope rests in God's promise of His strength to endure until reunited with our loved ones who have gone before us.

When Jesus saw the grieving of Mary and Martha as they, and the crowds, mourned the death of Lazarus, even our Lord cried (John 11:33). There are those who believe His tears were the result of seeing the unbelief and response of those around Him, or because He was bringing Lazarus back from a far better place to this fallen world. While these may have been factors, is it also possible that in His love and His humanity, He was touched by the grieving of His close friends. The tears of our Lord were replaced with the joy brought about by His raising Lazarus from his tomb and He visibly gave a glimpse of His deity and demonstrated what we all have in Christ—victory over death!

Admittedly, there is much about the sovereignty of God and the free will of man that is beyond our comprehension. Questions arise that go beyond our ability to understand, particularly when the answers don't relieve heartbreaking pain caused by disaster. Some wonder why God doesn't simply end all pain and evil? The simple answer is that if He did, then He would have to eliminate people, the cause of evil.

Another question centers on why people, who are made in God's image, are still able to cause suffering? Why doesn't God stop the evil acts that inevitably cause innocent people to hurt and suffer? Again, the answers are profound in their simplicity— to do all of this would take away man's free will to choose.

My computer has a number of board games that I find enjoyable. Some allow me to select a skill level from basic to the more advanced. In one sense, I am "god" of my computer game selections. I can make selections whereby I am assured to win. I can even program audio announcements that compliment me and praise me for how good and great I am in mastering the game. However, I find these programmed gestures meaningless and no matter how many times I'm glorified by my computer, I find no pleasure or value in such orchestrated, predetermined comments. It's only when I have not pre-designed such praise that I feel any sense of accomplishment and meaning.

Admittedly, the above is a weak analogy, but it does illustrate that love, worship, and praise can only come as we are allowed to make choices. Forced love is not true love. God wants heartfelt genuine love, and obedience. He didn't create robotic people who are programmed to bring honor and glory to Him by His eliminating adversity. As said before, He receives glory and honor when we rise above the hardships and continue to praise Him in obedience, knowing that He is in control.

God created us and allows us to to choose and express true love. This includes the capability not to love even if that produces sin, suffering, and evil. God didn't create puppets; He created us in His image with a mind, intellect and the ability to choose to love, worship, and follow Him as our Lord.

This life with all its hardships is the result of a fallen and sin-cursed world around us that people experience. How we respond to the world is what is most important. We may not be able to control the situation and the results of living in this world, but we can control our reactions and focus upon Him who loves us and will carry us through such painful experiences.

No doubt, the effects of a sin-cursed world filled with hardships, tragedies, and painful circumstances would be despairing if the story ended with this curse. However, God tells us in the Bible that anyone willing to restore his or her relationship with Him via His sacrificed Son, Jesus, and obey Him in faith will one day be totally free from the effects of sin. Jesus Christ came not simply to judge but to free sinners from the harmful effects of this curse. "So you see, just as death came into the world through a man, now the resurrection from the dead has begun through another man. *Just as everyone dies because we all belong to Adam, everyone who belongs to Christ will be given new life*" (1 Corinthians 15:21-22). God promises to someday lift the curse forever and we can be confident that as His children our lives will be spent in an eternal new home akin to his good and perfect original creation.

Suffering for Christ

> *Since they persecuted me [Jesus], naturally they*
> *will persecute you.*   —JOHN 15:20

Suffering for Christ is another possible source of hardship associated with being identified as a Christian and a follower of Christ. Such suffering varies from extreme to mild. This comes in various forms: discrimination, criticism, slander, humiliation, being ostracized, etc. Most recently, adhering to Biblical and Christian values may result in job loss, violation of laws, or forms of legal action. In many countries, it may be extreme resulting in physical pain, imprisonment, or even death.

Interestingly, recently American followers of Christ have encountered suffering for taking their Christian faith into the workplace or the educational system. This seldom occurred in our country's past. Sadly, though, this is rapidly changing due largely to the efforts of various activist groups. They have portrayed Christians as intolerant, narrow-minded, exclusive, and discriminatory. Unfortunately, our legal system has responded to restrict and, in some cases, prohibit Christianity reaching outside of the church walls. It is not uncommon today for individuals who take a stand for their faith in Christ and who speak or implement Biblical principles to be singled out and punished. This is a form of suffering for Christ.

So, how does God view such suffering? Jesus was very clear when he said, "Blessed are you when people insult you, persecute you and falsely say all kinds of evil against you because of me" (Matthew 5:11-12; NIV). Be happy about it! Be very glad! For a great reward awaits you in heaven. And, remember, the ancient prophets were persecuted in the same way."

Contrary to Jesus' teaching, we tend to be surprised and react when such suffering occurs as mentioned above. We want to react and strike back. However, Jesus' assumption was that as His followers, we naturally would encounter persecution. What Jesus is saying is that it is unnatural for us not to be persecuted and suffer. We should expect it, but all too often we are angered, hurt, pray for deliverance, or make plans to rebel and launch a counter offensive. Don't misunderstand; we need to be sensitive and involved to protect our faith, but we shouldn't be surprised. Rather, we should have a sense of urgency to participate in the Great Commission.

All this suggests that if we're not encountering persecution perhaps our faith is a closely guarded secret. If so, we may have a bigger problem. "Everyone who acknowledges me publicly here on earth, I will also acknowledge before my Father in heaven; but everyone who denies me here on earth, I will also deny before my Father in heaven" (Matthew 10:32-33).

No one claiming to be a follower of Christ would ever verbally deny Jesus; however actual behavior and actions often belie words and deny Jesus His rightful and visible place in the lives of many professing Christians. Jesus said in Matthew 7:20, "Just as you can identify a tree by its fruit, so you can identify people by their actions." Its noteworthy that He follows this teaching by saying that not everyone who calls Him, "Lord, Lord…will enter the Kingdom of heaven." It's sad that many well-meaning Christians who would sacrifice their lives for Christ if it ever came to such a necessity shrink from mentioning Jesus at the workplace for fear of repercussion.

A visiting Christian pastor from China recently toured the country and met with a group of pastors in our area. At the conclusion of his presentation, he was asked how we in this country could be praying for him and the church in China. His response surprised the group, "Please pray that the persecution will continue!" His message was that suffering creates a dependency that goes beyond the abilities and resources of people. At such time, people turn to God and faith flourishes.

Suffering for Christ in many cases is optional. At least in this country, it may or may not be forced upon us as believers. Unfortunately, many avoid public identification with Jesus for fear of offending or being politically incorrect and risking their careers. This is a view contrary to Scripture and in direct opposition to God's mission and the Great Commission! This world's message of toleration is a dangerous posture and one not taken lightly by God.

Discipline of God

A third potential source of hardships may come via God's disciplining us as His children.

> Don't make light of the Lord's discipline; and don't give up when He corrects you. For the Lord disciplines those He loves. —HEBREWS 12:5-6

> No discipline is enjoyable while it is happening— it's painful! But afterward there will be a peaceful harvest of right living for those who are trained in this way. —HEBREWS 12:11

> Don't reject the Lord's discipline and don't be upset when He corrects you; for the Lord corrects those He loves, just as a father corrects a child in whom He delights. —PROVERBS 3:11-12

God's discipline carries with it a constructive purpose that shapes our character toward godliness. God's children are special and His love is far greater than we can ever imagine. His love prompts Him to discipline for godliness sake to move us along in our journey to become more Christlike.

The key question is, how do we submit and "humble [ourselves] before God" (James 4:7) during times of discipline, especially when the hardship created is by our own wrongdoing? Surely this doesn't mean we become angry with God or accuse Him of injustice when difficult circumstances enter our lives. Admittedly, our initial response may be an emotional outcry defending ourselves, but this should be short-lived. Our focus should return to God as our loving Father refining us as He deems.

It's more serious when someone allows anger and sorrow toward God to continue for a long period, even for a lifetime. Such an attitude amounts to a charge or grudge against God and actually is rebellion and falls far short of submitting and humbling ourselves before God. We do need God's strength and uplifting during such times of adversity. God's Word gives us the solution, "Humble yourselves, therefore, under God's mighty hand that He may lift you up in due time" (1 Peter 5:6 NIV).

One facet of humbling ourselves before God is to admit that we have much room for growth in our character. In God's infinite wisdom, He knows exactly the extent of adversity we can endure. His Word assures of this, "He [God] will not allow the temptation to be more than you can stand. When you are tempted, He will show you a way out so that you can endure" (1 Corinthians 10:13). God knows well what we need and the extent of our endurance to accomplish His purpose in our lives.

Some mistakenly assume that adversity is a sign that God has forsaken them when, in fact, it may be God's love that results in His discipline and grace in calling them to repentance.

God's discipline may result in our being allowed to suffer for "reaping what we sow" when engaging in some sinful act or practice. God is a loving and forgiving God, but sin does have consequences. Such things as excessive debt, greed, addictions, acting apart from God, all of these may result in hardship or crisis. God's discipline may allow sin to run its course resulting in or creating severe hardship. There are negative consequences for acting in an ungodly manner.

The Greek word, *paideian*, translated in our English Bible as "discipline," combines the thoughts of chastening with training and education as one would instruct a child. It pictures suffering as positive, to teach us something. God loves us therefore He disciplines us. No circumstance is beyond His control and use to accomplish His purpose in our life. It's noteworthy that the discipline passages in Hebrews 12 are presented as words of encouragement from God.

As noted above, God's discipline is a corrective action brought about by sin. It is important to understand that in the midst of reaping what we've sown, we have a proper perspective of guilt. God's discipline has at its core purpose restoration. Care needs to be taken to understand "condemnation" and "conviction." Guilt over sin will typically result in one of these two conditions.

So now there is no condemnation for those who belong to Christ Jesus.   —ROMANS 8:1

But if we confess our sins to him, he is faithful and just to forgive us our sins and to cleanse us from all wickedness.   —1 JOHN 1:9

THE TWO FACES OF GUILT

Condemnation	Conviction
Depression	Confession
Self-defeated	Repentance
Rendered useless	Forgiveness
Self-focused	Focused on God's love and promise
Defeated by sin	Victory over sin
Spiral downward	Uplifted
Driven from God	Restoration

Guilt over sin that leads to conviction and repentance is good;

guilt that spins off into condemnation is not good and can have a disastrous result. One of the devil's most effective weapons in the lives of Christians is to render them shipwrecked and useless for God's purpose by guilt and self-condemnation over some sin. It's bad enough to experience the hardship caused by sin, but even more to emerge with a spirit of condemnation ignoring God's love and forgiveness leading to restoration.

It's always good and proper to look within ourselves at times of hardship and adversity to evaluate what part we had in its creation. Also, counseling from spiritually mature believers who speak the truth in love and provide Scriptural guidance can be most helpful.

Training in Godliness

Training in godliness is another potential source of hardship in the life of a Christian.

God often allows or causes tests and trials to reveal the extent of and to strengthen our faith in moving us toward godliness. It helps to understand the nature of such challenges. Surely this is not to inform God about the legitimacy and extent of our faith; He already knows this. Then what is the purpose of the test or trial? If not for God, then it must be for us. In this regard, the hardship may reveal and strengthen our faith and bring honor to and glorify Him. First Peter 1:7 speaks of this when addressing suffering, "that the proof of your faith...though it is proved by fire, may be found unto praise and glory and honor at the revelation of Jesus Christ" (ASV).

This possible source of what might be considered a hardship differs from God's discipline. Discipline is a corrective action caused by sin. We bring it on ourselves and reap what we sow. God therefore may discipline via some hardship to correct us. Apart from His discipline, He may also use hardships to train and move us toward godliness and equip us for greater use. Such trials are not connected or caused by sin.

If you're like most, there were some unique lessons learned as a youth by active involvement in some rigorous team sport. Few other activities teach such important life lessons as discipline, sacrifice, or endurance with physical pain that builds character and achieves goals. Likewise, God may choose to use hardships to replace pride, fear, and self-centeredness with humility, dependence upon Him, forgiveness, and increased faith. God may have great assignments that first require our strengthening; therefore hardships may be preparatory in nature.

We avoid thinking about situations where God might allow or even cause what the world would classify as horrible adversities. However, God may choose to do just that in order to accomplish something far greater than we could imagine. Consider how awful and terrifying it was for God to allow His only Son, Jesus, to be mocked, beaten, and crucified on a cross. What good could possibly come out of that unimaginable horror? The salvation of mankind. Some adversities and their resulting good are best viewed in retrospect.

Great hearts are made by great troubles. Often, God allows trying circumstances as opportunities for growth and the exercising of faith and endurance so that He may be glorified. What makes a more dramatic impression—one who in the midst of wealth, health, and abundance talks about how good God is—or, one who in the midst of failing health and trying circumstances continues to praise God and witness to His greatness? The answer is obvious. Nothing honors Him more than the unquestioned confidence of our hearts when everything seems thoroughly against us.

Charles Spurgeon, the legendary minister during the 1800s, experienced much suffering during his lifetime. His perspective toward such hardships reveals God's greater purpose, "Most of the grand truths of God have to be learned by trouble; they must be burned into us with the hot iron of affliction, otherwise we shall not truly receive them. Great hearts can only be made by great troubles. I believe there is no place where we can learn so much and have so much light cast upon Scripture as we do in the furnace. Read a verse during tranquil times and you will make nothing of it; be put inside the furnace and you will understand more than you ever would absent the fire of the furnace! We do not grow strong in faith on sunshiny days! Suffering and hardships make us complete and teaches us truths we would otherwise never learn."[17]

Training in godliness includes testing that reveals who or what is our source of strength and dependence. God's definition of an idol is anything that takes the rightful place of God in our lives. These may be ill-advised easy credit and debt, financial savings, human effort, insurance, parents, health and physical strength, etc. God may cause or allow trials to come into our life in order to identify such idols and display how foolish and inadequate they are, and how misguided we are for depending upon them rather than upon God.

Jeremiah 2:10-13 points out how ridiculous it is to trade faith in God for idols, "Has anyone ever heard of anything as strange as this? Has any nation ever traded its gods for new ones, even though they are not gods at all? Yet my people have exchanged their glorious God for worthless idols! The heavens are shocked at such a thing and shrink back in horror and dismay says the Lord." If God and all of His heaven are shocked and dismayed and think it strange to depend upon something other than God, then should we be surprised when God allows or causes events and trials to come into our lives that reveal how wrong this is?

Each of us can be challenged with a sobering question, "Is Jesus enough?" If God were to allow everything to be taken away that we value—everything—would Jesus be enough?

Training in godliness also addresses a misguided approach prevalent today among some who design and implement their own agenda and then ask God to bless or, if wrong, to stop it.

We are an impatient society and our impatience has carried over into our relationship with God. Seeking God's lead has become a lost discipline. It's just easier simply to tell God, "I'm going to go ahead and do this and if you don't like it, you can stop it or prevent me from doing it." While this sounds good and may even be cloaked with telling God how much this will benefit Him, in truth it is self-centered heresy. The servant does not tell the Master; the Master tells the servant! God does not need our help, but only our obedience to follow Him, His agenda, and His activities.

God condemned the Israelites for their planning apart from Him: "You make plans that are contrary to Mine... For without consulting Me [you have acted.]" The results of this human effort were *"[You] will be ashamed, He will not help you. Instead He will disgrace you"* (Isaiah 30:1-5).

The cost of discipleship and following Christ

The cost of being a devoted follower of Christ, a disciple, carries with it a cost. This is considered by many to be a source of hardship that few are willing to pay. This is in a different category from being persecuted for Christ. As discussed, being persecuted for Christ results in your identification with Christ and suffering as a consequence of being identified as a Christian. At its extreme is martyrdom and, at its least, is discrimination or simply being unpopular.

Being a disciple and committed follower of Christ includes choices. Those choices might carry costs that from the world's perspective are classified as hardships. These hardships are the cost of patterning your life and basing your decisions with what is pleasing to God. This impacts your values, priorities, how you spend your time, finances, career choices, possessions, family relationships, what you do or don't do—in other words, your entire life.

I'm reminded of a taped interview with Elizabeth Elliot,

widow of Jim Elliot, martyred missionary in the jungles of Ecuador. She tells the story of encountering a lady who had just heard her tell the story of living in the jungle in South America attempting to make contact with an unreached Indian tribe. The lady approached Elizabeth and told her how impressed she was that Elizabeth went to the jungle to live, but how she could never do that with all "those snakes, spiders, and other wild animals down there!" Elizabeth calmly responded, "Do you really think that I liked to live among all those snakes and spiders? I dislike them as much as anyone, but that was where God called us and we followed his guiding even in the midst of snakes and spiders." The choices the Elliots made brought challenges and hardships (and eventual martyrdom to Jim), but they were the right choices and bore much fruit as history revealed.

Most likely our choices will not include going to the jungle or be life threatening. However, the critical issue is the same. Should we follow Christ's lead or opt for a different and more pleasing and acceptable course? Frequently, that course may seem attractive and hold significant benefits from the world's perspective but is it God's way? Choosing Christ's way for many might seem to be filled with hardship and potential suffering. This view comes from the world's definition of "hardship" which considers any event that jeopardizes comfort, security, health, career, etc., as adversity.

J. Oswald Sanders in his classic book, *Spiritual Leadership*, commented on the high cost of discipleship. "Scars are the authentic marks of faithful discipleship and true spiritual leadership. Willingness to renounce personal preferences, to sacrifice legitimate and natural desires for the sake of His kingdom, will characterize those marked out by God for positions of influence in His work."[18]

From the world's perspective, there is a cost and hardship in following Christ. However, we know that living in obedience to our Father God and striving to be Christlike in our choices in life is a fulfilling adventure. Our companionship and walk with Christ overshadows the costs and defeats the many evils and negative forces of the world.

We glory in Him and count it all joy!

The consequences of bad decisions or actions

Well known author Robert Louis Stevenson (1850-1894) commenting on questionable life decisions said, "Sooner or later, we all have to sit down to a banquet of consequences."[19] We have to admit that many of life's hardships are of our own making. Most often they are the unintended consequences of wrong or foolish decisions or actions. By themselves, they may not be a sin or violate any Biblical principle. Irrespective of the best of intentions, there are times when we have to confess, "I was wrong." At such times, we have to take ownership, admit our mistake, seek forgiveness if applicable, correct any damage, avoid rationalizing our mistake, or blaming others or God.

No doubt, all of us have been subjected to this possible source of hardship. I'm reminded of the successful businessman who was asked to identify the key to his success. He responded, "Making good decisions." He was then asked how he learned to make good decisions. He replied, "By making bad decisions."

Life consists of decisions and choices; some will be good and others not so good and those may bring about adversity. Learn from them, press on being more thoughtful and do better the next time.

The judgment of God

The judgment of God is not commonly considered as a possible source of hardship in today's world, but it is real in Scripture.

God judged nations and people due to their sinful behavior.

One only has to consider the history of the Israelites, Sodom and Gomorrah, and Babylon to realize this truth in Scripture. As God blesses nations, rulers, and people, He also removes His blessing, and hardships come with his judgmental actions.

America is one of the most blessed nations in history. However, one has to wonder how long God will be patient with a country so engrossed in sin. The recent blatant attempts to remove all public references to God outside of churches are heresy and a departure from our Judeo-Christian foundation and history.

The late Christian philosopher Francis A. Schaeffer noted America's trend toward ungodliness in his book *The Great Evangelical Disaster:* "There is only one perspective we can have of the post-Christian world of our generation: an understanding that our culture and our country deserves to be under the wrath of God. It will not do to say the United States is God's country in some special way. It will not do to cover up the difference between the consensus today and the Christian consensus that prevailed sixty years ago. The last few generations have trampled upon the truth of the Bible and all that those truths have brought forth."[20] Unfortunately, the present generation has continued the trend away from godliness.

There are those who would argue that America is experiencing God's progressive judgment. They believe God is allowing a progressive number of national crises and disasters in order to turn us back to Himself. The horrible terrorist attacks of 9/11 generated an immediate reaction from various circles for God's help. Church attendance mushroomed as the public sought answers and assurances. Unfortunately, these were short-lived and failed to result in any sustained cultural change. This doesn't suggest that God originated and caused such a crisis; however, could God have stopped it? Certainly. Did He? No. Then it is safe to conclude that God allowed the crisis. Could there have been a purpose? We must not dismiss the possibility that God is allowing events and crises to get our attention and draw us back to Himself.

One of the most revolutionary truths is that God is ever-present, engaged, and at work in and around us. He is not detached and far away awaiting on us to summon Him only when needed. Just as God was well aware of the condition of countries and empires in Biblical times, so is He today. Is it possible that the financial meltdown of Wall Street and the economic distress of the past few years is God's judgment on the materialistic trend of our culture? No doubt, many innocent Christians were affected by this national hardship. It is noteworthy that the last great Christian revival in America occurred in the late 1920s with the Great Depression and collapse of the financial system! A lesson not learned might be a lesson repeated!

Whenever God's judgment occurs, people, Christian and non-Christian, suffer. Our responsibility as His children is to be faithful. It's interesting to note that the culture during the time of Jesus' earthly ministry was as wicked as today's. Jesus' message was focused on the individual and his or her repentance, reconciliation, and preparation for the coming of God's kingdom.

Jesus knew that the key to changing a society and culture lies in changing the hearts of individuals. Failure to do this only results in temporary change. There is a lesson for us and we need to be focused and actively involved in God's mission and the Great Commission.

Chapter 5: Where Does This Stuff Come From?

Summary Points for Reflection

1. God can use challenging experiences for His purpose in our lives or the world. This, however, doesn't mean that He causes or orchestrates each and every crisis.

2. It is helpful to identify the possible sources of hardship in order to discern what may or may not be God's activity. They are:

   - Life's troubles in the fallen world
   - Suffering for Christ
   - Discipline of God
   - Training in godliness
   - The cost of discipleship and following Christ
   - The consequences of bad or foolish decisions and actions
   - God's judgment of a nation

3. God's original creation was good and perfect in every respect. Disasters and hardships are the consequences of man's free will to choose to sin.

4. Christians have no supernatural umbrella shielding them from this world's hardships. Christians however do have a great and loving God that will provide His abundant resources during times of crisis. Our faith and hope rests not in our ability to understand, but rather our trust in God's promises.

5. We may not be able to control the effects of living in a fallen world, but we can control our reaction and focus upon God who loves us and will carry us through each painful experience.

6. God's discipline is motivated by His love and is for correction and training, not punishment. He may allow hardships in order to strengthen our faith and character in moving us toward godliness.

7. Humbling ourselves before God is admitting that we have much room for growth in our character.

8. It's good to look within ourselves at times of hardship to determine what part we may have had in its creation.

9. Being a follower of Christ includes choices; many of which may, from the world's perspective, seem foolish or be viewed as hardships.

Chapter 5: Questions for Meditation & Discussion

1. As you reflect back over your life, what category would you place the adversities and challenges that you have experienced to date? Note: Some hardships serve multiple purposes.

    • Life's normal troubles, trials, and consequences of living in a fallen world

    • Suffering for Christ

    • Discipline of God

    • Training in godliness

    • The costs of discipleship and following Christ

    • Consequences of bad or foolish decisions or actions

    • The judgment of God

2. Read the definition of "faith" given in Hebrews 11:1 and

note the phrase "assurance about things we cannot see." What things can't we see that provide a foundation for us to exercise faith?

3. How would you respond to someone who commented, "I can't believe in or accept a God who would allow so much pain and suffering and bad things to happen in this world. If there is a God, He must not love us or not be very powerful!"

4. What can we learn from the Apostle Paul's view of his adversity as revealed in Philippians 1:12-14?

5. What can we learn from the warnings in 2 Timothy 4:3 and the condemnation by Jesus in Matthew 15:9? What kind of present day teaching "tickles people's ears"?

6. What are the teachings and truths in the following verses?

> John 16:33
>
> 2 Timothy 3:12
>
> James 1:3

7. Charles Spurgeon said, "Most of the grand truths of God have to be learned by trouble; they must be burned into us with the hot iron of affliction." Do you agree or disagree? Explain your answer.

8. Review the Scriptural characteristics of a "disciple" and rate yourself beside each indicating "O = Okay", "M = Marginal", or "NW = Needs Work."

_____ Honors God by doing whatever is on God's heart and mind. 1 Samuel 2:35

_____ Glorifies God. 1 Corinthians 10:31; Colossians 3:17

_____ Embodies integrity. Genesis 6:9

_____ Embraces truth. Ephesians 4:25

_____ Does things God's ways. Isaiah 55:8-9; Psalms 25:4, 27:11

_____ Is trustworthy, honest, and faultless. 1 Thessalonians 2:10

_____ Demonstrates wisdom. Matthew 7:24-27

_____ Abides, holds fast, obeys, and lives in accordance with God's Word. John 8:31

_____ Exhibits unselfish love. John 13:34-35; Matthew 22:37-39

_____ Has a high degree of commitment. Matthew 10:37-39

_____ Exercises spiritual gift(s). 1 Timothy 4:14

_____ Bears fruit. John 15:5, 8

_____ Participates in the Great Commission. Matthew 28:19-20

_____ Serves as Christ's ambassador. 2 Corinthians 5:20; John 20:21

- Select two of your "Needs Work" items and describe what you can begin to do to improve them.

- Is it possible that God can orchestrate or allow events to occur in your life in order to develop or improve any of the characteristics listed above? How might He do this?

CHAPTER SIX

IS THIS GOD'S WILL?

A re all hardships God's will?

A family loses a precious little one at birth.

A parent is taken away leaving a survivor with small children and no means of support.

A business fails; a home is lost by foreclosure; marriages split; jobs are lost; cancer strikes.

The list is endless.

Where does the will of God fit or apply in these situations? Is everything that happens, good or bad, God's will and desire? Has God's will become the Christian's default to explain life's negative events? If an event or situation is characterized as being God's will, does this imply that God intended and caused it to happen? What does this say about God? What reaction does it produce from parents when you tell them it was God's will that a drunk driver killed their child?

No examination of hardship would be complete without undertaking a discussion of God's will. It is important to have a basic understanding of God's will; what it is, and, perhaps more importantly, what it isn't; and how it is related to hardships causing suffering. There is a general lack of understanding related to the truth of God's will and this has created much confusion and misuse. The fact is that we have complicated this entire matter.

God often mistakenly is blamed for a variety of negative events under the pretext that everything that happens is His will. This is understandable and comes from acknowledging God's sovereignty and power to mean that every event in the world, good or bad, is His desire or will. Obviously in God's omniscience there are no surprises. He knows well what is happening now and what will happen in the future. In addition, His omnipotence certainly enables Him to control or to intervene as He chooses. However, such foreknowledge and power does not give us license to blame or accuse God for every negative catastrophe or hardship and simply conclude that all are His will.

It is true that God has, can, and may send adversity and various trials, but, as discussed elsewhere, hardships and suffering may find their source in a number of different causes. It's important to be reminded that God did not create puppets, but instead gave humans the ability to choose. In general, this is what is meant by "free will." Some say that this ability to act according to man's choice is God's "permissive will"; however this often results in painful consequences.

Some might ask why God doesn't eliminate all evil, pain, and suffering, at least for Christians. After all, if He is all-powerful, then why doesn't He rid the world of everything that is bad? From a human viewpoint, this makes sense. Upon further consideration, it overlooks another important implication of such a humanitarian action: what about the consequences of sin? All the bad things we may want eliminated find their origin in our ability to choose. Some choices may include sinning. Therefore, if God is to eliminate all that is "bad," then either our ability to choose must be significantly limited or taken away, or the results of sinning must be removed. These have further implications. If there are no consequences of sin, then there is no need of a Savior; if our ability to think independently and make choices is absent, then we become far less than what God created.

Since God is all-powerful and loves His children, one might think that at least a loving God should eliminate all the bad things from the lives of Christians. Becoming a Christian, therefore, would guarantee a life immune from anything painful. Again, while this sounds attractive on the surface, it has some serious failings. Recognizing that many "bad things" come as a result of our "bad choices," then, most obvious, is the requirement that our ability to choose must be altered in order to prevent us from choosing wrongly.

Also, removing all the negative events from Christians' lives dilutes or destroys genuine faith and choosing to believe in a need for a Savior. Assurance of the absence of pain and hardships would encourage "signing up" to become a Christian and gaining a life of perpetual ease with only positive experiences. Correction and training in righteousness would be annulled and the consequences of sin would disappear. Repentance and cultivating a life of dependency upon God would no longer be needed. While this certainly would be in keeping with the world's focus on comfort and pleasure—it is not an acceptable motivation or basis for becoming a Christian.

A Closer Look At God's "Will"

Admittedly, times of hardships and suffering can create questions. No doubt, many situations are the will and desire of God, but, just as important, many are not. It's easy to call everything God's will without realizing what we're saying and more importantly what it says about God. A basic understanding of God's will is helpful in this regard.

This starts by a closer examination of the Bible's use of the word "will." The Bible's New Testament is an English translation from the original Greek language. There are times when English cannot capture the full meaning of the Greek. We find this true for our one English word "will."

Forms of two Greek words, *thelo* and *boulomai*, are often translated into the one English word "will." Some translations may also use the words "plan" or "purpose," but all of these come from some form of these same two Greek words. These words have very different meanings. Understanding each helps us to properly interpret various verses expressing God's "will."

The first Greek word often translated to the English word "will" is from forms of *thelo*. Examples of its use are found in the following verses:

- "So then do not be foolish, but understand what the *will* of the Lord is" (Ephesians 5:17 NASB).

- "He made known to us the mystery of His *will* according to his kind intention ..." (Ephesians 1:9)

- "Not everyone who calls me 'Lord, Lord!' will enter the kingdom of heaven. Only those who actually do the *will* of My Father in heaven will enter." (Jesus speaking in Matthew 7:21)

- Other verses speak of God's *will* that all should be saved. (1 Timothy 2:4)

Thelo is a Greek word used to describe a desire of the heart or to want. It appears sixty-four times in Scripture; sixty-two as "will"; once as "desire"; and once as "pleasure." *Thelo* speaks of God's desire for what He wants in the lives of His children; what He desires us to do and be and how He urges us to act. He may "desire" us to be or act in a certain way but allows us to choose. In this regard, it can be viewed as God's "permissive will." God communicates His *thelo*, but in our God-allowed freedom, we are permitted to choose our actions—some which may not be good or in accord with His desire or *thelo* will.

In contrast, the second Greek word often translated into our one English word "will" is much stronger and appears in the Greek as forms of *boulomai*. Some Greek forms of this are translated and appear as God's "will", "plan"; "intention;" or "as planned." This word conveys a decided absolute intention, a determination, a pre-determined decision. In this regard, God's *boulomai* is certain, unconditional and will be accomplished. We see this translated to the English words "will" or "plan" forty-eight times in Scripture. Examples are found in the following verses:

- *"But God knew what would happen, and His prearranged plan was carried out when Jesus was betrayed..."* —ACTS 2:23

- *"But everything they did was determined beforehand according to Your will."* —ACTS 4:28

- *"Furthermore, because we are united with Christ, we have received an inheritance from God, for He chose us in advance, and He makes everything work out according to his plan.* —EPHESIANS 1:11

- Hebrews 6:17 speaks of the "unchangeable things of His *will*".

As is obvious, the stronger forms of the Greek word *boulomai* differ significantly from *thelo*. Whereas one is permissive, a desire, and conditional; the other is absolute, unchangeable and sovereign. Understanding this, we can see the potential for confusion by using one English word these two Greek words. We routinely see in our English Bible the use of words such as "will", "plan", "purpose", or "intent" without understanding their meaning in the original Greek language. This often leads to a misunderstanding of God's "will." Examples of this are:

- *"Never stop praying. Be thankful in all circumstances for this is God's will for you who belong to Christ Jesus."*
  — 1 THESSALONIANS 5:17-18

On the surface this verse can be problematic if you view this as God's sovereign pre-determined "will" which will not and cannot be violated. We may choose not to pray or be thankful. If so, what does that then say about God's "will?" Understanding that the English word as used in this verse is a translation from the Greek "thelo" provides understanding. It is God's "desire" that we never stop praying and giving thanks, but not His absolute "will."

- *"[God] desires (a form of "thelo") all men to be saved and to understand the truth."* —1 TIMOTHY 2:4

While this is God's desire, in practice and in respect of man's ability to choose, notwithstanding that it is God that is the driving and saving agent in the salvation process, we know that some will not be saved.

God's sovereign "will" is unconditional and will be fulfilled; however, many of His "desires" may not be accomplished. This raises the question: Why does God even have a *thelo* will? If God has a desire, then why doesn't He exercise His power and by enforcement assure all His desires are met? Why doesn't God make His desires and pleasures stronger and part of his irresistible and unchangeable *boulomai* will and plan? There is no clear answer other than as mentioned earlier to do so impacts the ability to choose and without choice there can be no genuine love, honor or worship.

Understanding that one aspect of God's will is His *thelo* (desire), we must then accept the fact that God is purposeful. He may use and allow hardships or the results of adversities to refine us into that which He desires for us: godliness. In this sense, one could say that some hardships are part of God's *thelo* or permissive will.

Having said that, it is important that we understand that God finds no pleasure in seeing us suffer or bearing the consequences of living in this fallen world. His pleasure is found when we choose His ways and work toward Christlikeness. It is not God's *thelo* (will) for children to die of disease, for innocent people to lose their lives at the hand of criminals, or other tragedies and catastrophes—all these and other negative consequences came about when sin entered the world. God can use these for His good purposes and in His love can provide super-natural resources. To accuse God arbitrarily for all such events is simply wrong and lacks an understanding and knowledge of God.

Finding and Following God's Will

Following God's will and pleasing Him should be a priority for every Christian. Living a life with decisions and actions in accordance with His will is not a mystery. When we speak of finding God's will as related to decisions or directions, we are speaking about God's *thelo*, His wants or desires for our lives.

Many of the problems centered on the search for God's will come more from a lack of understanding. In practice, more problems arise from lack of obedience in following God's will than from finding God's will. God's desire for how we should live our lives is not a secret nor is His criteria for decision-making. If a problem exists, it is with us, not Him.

Some become paralyzed in their consuming search for God's will. In their sincere desire to be absolutely certain that they follow His will regarding major decisions or opportunities, they may become frustrated and at a standstill unable to act for fear of stepping outside of God's will.

Related to the above group are those who go to extremes and take each and every decision of life and attempt to apply specific Biblical justification to every decision, or find some means of spiritual guidance or a sign to assure their actions are God's will. Such behavior, even though motivated by a sincere desire to be obedient, presents problems and challenges as Scripture is silent on many of life's circumstances. This can create uncertainty, tentative action or half-hearted commitments. It may result in a lifetime of standing on the sidelines of life never sure if or when to act or become a useful instrument for God's use. Satan delights in such an attitude!

Many sincere folks go to extreme lengths and resort to some rather bizarre tests to assure themselves of God's will. A story is told about a lady struggling with a decision about whether to take an evangelical trip that involved flying. She agonized for days searching for God's will. One morning she awoke and looked at her digital clock that displayed 7:47. She believed this was a direct sign from God that she should fly on a 747 jet. One would think our Biblical commission to go and share the gospel is a far better reason versus seeking God's will by a clock or some Magic 8 Ball device.

Sometimes the stories are humorous (and probably exaggerated). In desperation, a businessman whose company was struggling sought God's will. He randomly opened his Bible and felt God spoke to him when he saw on the page facing him, "Chapter 11." He went forward into Chapter 11 bankruptcy claiming God told him to do this! Using this lucky dip method for guidance is not recommended.

Whether these stories, and others, are true is doubtful, but they illustrate the extremes and man-made exercises some invent to discover what they believe to be God's will. Admittedly, God can use any instrument He chooses to communicate, but depending upon and trusting in questionable external signs is lacking Biblically and is certainly the exception, not the rule.

Sadly, there are those who manipulate or wrongly use God's will as justification or a defense of their own personal agenda apart from God, and contrary to Scripture. Such individuals are prone to label their decisions or actions by proclaiming, "This is God's will for me." Often times, they have no Scriptural basis or leading and have not prayerfully sought godly direction and simply make this statement and proceed with their own personal agenda.

Similar to this group are those who go through life doing whatever they desire with the attitude, "If God doesn't want me to do this, or if this isn't His will, He will stop me." No doubt, God can and often does stop us, but habitually following either of these approaches routinely for life's decisions is not an acceptable Scriptural process. Just saying this is God's will doesn't automatically make it true, nor is our going about life and acting apart from God expecting Him to step in and call a halt if the act is against His will. In reality, this is a self-centered approach disguised as being God-centered.

The above is particularly rampant among those who ascribe to the open/closed door approach to following God's will. How often have you heard, "God opened the door and I'm proceeding. If He doesn't want me doing it, He will close it." This overlooks the fact that Satan, the master of deceit, can also open doors that may appear attractive. It also presumes that any so-called open door can be walked through without committing such to prayer and seeking God's guidance. All too often, the open door approach is more self-centered and typically is governed by worldly desires versus what God may want.

The open door approach also overlooks or disregards Biblical criteria for evaluating so-called opportunities. Who defines "opportunity?" In essence, the person interprets the opportunity as God-given, and expects God to act. God may choose not to close the door and thus allow the person to bear the consequences of such actions apart from Him. How sad it is when one follows this approach without Biblically evaluating the action and prayerfully seeking God's direction, and then the mistakenly perceived opportunity results in a crisis or failure. While some realize their error, others may be prone to blame God and take no accountability for their disobedience. Be cautious and discerning when so-called opportunities come into your path. No doubt, God may provide genuine opportunities and open doors, but don't jump without discerning and seeking His guidance.

Another popular approach is the pro and con or balance sheet approach. This is used effectively and frequently in business situations evaluating costs versus benefits. However, a problem occurs when we take this secular decision-making process and apply it spiritually. When seeking God's will, it is a mistake to make a comparative list of all the pluses and minuses for an action under consideration. If the positives outweigh the negatives, then an assumption is made that this represents and confirms God's will.

The error in this approach is who determines pro from con and right from wrong? We tend to forget that what may appear to be positive from a human standpoint, may, in fact, be negative from God's perspective, and vice versa. Even those who do not believe in God use the pro and con approach as it is entirely decided upon by man. We need to be reminded that God's thoughts are not man's thoughts and God's ways are much higher than man's. (Isaiah 55:8) There may be times when the only pro reason is a special calling from God, and the con side is filled with all the world's reasons why this is a bad decision. In such cases, with assurance that it is God's calling, the pro trumps the con. Keep in mind that Moses, too, had many reasons and excuses to avoid delivering God's message to the Egyptian Pharaoh.

The pro and con approach would never have worked for the Apostle Paul. Even he admitted in 1 Corinthians 4:10, "Our dedication to Christ makes us look like fools." Paul's dedication and leading was from God and not man. This is evident throughout his many epistles. A prominent example is found in 1 Corinthians 2:13-15 as Paul explained that he didn't come to the Corinthians with human words or wisdom. He continued to talk about how this sounds foolish to those who cannot understand it. Paul's perspective, coupled with the fact that God's ways are far different than man's, renders the pro and con approach lacking, if not misleading, when used to identify God's will.

This is not to suggest that God cannot give specific direction via his Holy Spirit by his Word, circumstances, the church, or other godly counselors. However, in general, when Scripture is silent about an act or the specifics surrounding a decision, then it is helpful to ask questions that attempt to examine the action in line with general Scriptural principles.

God's vs. the World's Criteria

There may be situations when a selection must be made between two different alternatives and both appear favorable. A decision is complicated when both options appear to be equal, are in compliance with Biblical criteria, and God seems to be "silent" and not giving any specific direction as to what choice to make. During such times and facing such options, then God allows us to choose as we wish. There are those who agonize over such situations and may become frozen and unable to act. While genuine in their longing to please and follow God, they fail to understand that if specific guidance as mentioned above is lacking, and if the decision meets the Scriptural criteria, then whatever they select between the two options will comply with God's will.

Throughout the Bible, God has revealed much to us about His will. Scripture contains examples of God leading individuals. He can be very specific with individuals regarding decisions and directions; however God's expressed desired will is most often general in nature. The problem typically is not that we have difficulty knowing His will; the problem is we tend to ignore what He has already told us. Examples of God's stated will for our lives are:

1 Thessalonians 5:18	*Be thankful*
1 Thessalonians 4:3	*Be holy*
Philippians 2:13	*Do what is pleasing to God*
Colossians 4:2	*Devote yourselves to prayer*
John 15:5	*Abide in Him*
Psalm 40:8	*Be joyful*
Matthew 6:33	*Seek His kingdom*
Matthew 22:37-39	*Love God with all heart, soul, and mind*
2 Corinthians 5:20	*Be Christ's ambassador*
2 Peter 3:18	*Grow in grace and knowledge of our Lord*
1 Corinthians 10:31	*Do all for God's glory*

Unfortunately, many only give attention to following His will at times of decisions about key events of life. God desires that we live each day following His will. All of the characteristics listed above are His will. He has clearly communicated His desired will for us to be Christlike and bring Him honor and glory wherever we are, in whatever we're doing, whenever we can, and however is possible.

Following this line of thinking, we often ask the wrong questions. For example, one might be prone to focus entirely on asking God if a new job should be taken. Perhaps, it would be best to focus on how this will impact all the criteria given in Scripture that directly relates to our obedience and intimate relationship with God. In other words, if any option under consideration inhibits one's ability to be thankful, holy, pleasing to God, prayerful, joyful, or glorifying God, then it should be avoided.

God's criteria differs greatly from what the world values as reasons for or against pursuing a course of action. Typically the world places maximum value on self and how any action will hurt or enhance pleasure, money, advancement, appearance, possessions, security and safety, or status. None of these are found in God's desires.

If God wants you to be in another place, change your direction, or do something differently, you can rest assured He will get your attention. In Scripture, there is no doubt about what God wants or when He acts. There is no missing His intent. Our role is to stay close to Him and follow and act in obedience.

As mentioned above, it is sad that God's will typically is only focused upon when struggling with what is considered the "big" decisions of life. No doubt, these are times to seek God's guidance. However, God's desired will encompasses our entire life and that includes the smaller details. Many struggle to discover and follow God's will with these so-called big decisions, but their lives betray their sincerity and obedience in following God's will as communicated for all the other areas of their lives. Why should God reveal His will for what we consider the big decisions when we never follow His will on all His other desires for our lives?

God is sequential. He may wait on us to display our obedience and faith in the little things of life before guiding us or allowing us to move forward to greater assignments. It is distressing to hear individuals talk about wanting to follow God's will in certain matters while disregarding God's will in other areas. Most notable is being a godly husband or wife and a positive spiritual parenting influence for children.

God's will is not a cafeteria line where we Christians can pick and choose what suits us. This is presumptuous and an affront to God. Some ask for prayer to enable them to know and follow God's will in a decision about a new job offer or relocation, but their personal lives show no commitment or love for God,

His Word, or in their prayer life. In such situations one has to wonder why God would respond.

God's will and desire for our lives is no mystery or shrouded in some secret fashion in the Scriptures; nor is it only to be found in supernatural and bizarre signs. God's will is very clear and plain in His desire for each of His children to grow in a close and intimate, loving relationship with Him that translates into displaying Christlike behavior regardless of the situation. God loves us with an incredible love.

To repeat—the problem is not so much in knowing God's will as it is in following God's will.

Chapter 6: Is This God's Will?

Summary Points for Reflection

1. God often is mistakenly blamed for a variety of negative events under the pretext that everything that happens is His will.

2. It is important to be reminded that God did not create puppets, but instead gave humans the ability to choose.

3. Removing all the hardships and negative events from a Christian's life dilutes genuine love and destroys faith and belief in a need for a Savior.

4. God's will is clear and is no mystery or shrouded in some secret fashion in the Scriptures; nor is it only to be found in supernatural and bizarre signs. Following God's will and pleasing Him should be a priority for every Christian.

5. The problem is not that we have difficulty in identifying God's will and what pleases Him; the problem is we tend to ignore what He has already told us in the Bible.

6. God clearly communicates His specific desires for us. Biblical examples are to be thankful, holy, pleasing to God, prayerful, joyful, loving, and many other characteristics of Christlikeness.

7. God's will encompasses every aspect of our life and not just the "big" decisions. His will is not a cafeteria line for Christians to pick and choose what suits them.

8. God can and often does give specific guidance and direction, but many times He allows us to choose what we want conditioned upon satisfying all of His qualitative criteria.

9. God is sequential in that He may desire us to be faithful in the "little" things of life first before allowing us to move forward with greater assignments.

10. God's desire is for each of His children to grow in a close and intimate, loving relationship with Him that translates into displaying Christlike behavior regardless of the circumstance.

Chapter 6: Questions for Meditation & Discussion

1. What do you consider to be God's will for your life?

2. When faced with what appears to be a decision or opportunity and you want to make sure you follow God's will, describe what you would do in making this determination.

3. Review the many desires of God as mentioned in the following verses. Indicate those that need work in your life and what you can do to improve.

- 1 Thessalonians 5:18 "Be thankful"

- 1 Thessalonians 4:3 "Be holy"

- Philippians 2:13 "Do what is pleasing to God"

- Colossians 4:2 "Devote yourselves to prayer"

- John 15:5 "Abide in Him"

- Psalm 40:8 "Be joyful"

- Matthew 6:33 "Seek His kingdom"

- Matthew 22:37-39 "Love God with all heart, soul, and mind"

- 2 Corinthians 5:20 "Be Christ's ambassador"

- 2 Peter 3:18 "Grow in grace and knowledge of our Lord"

- 1 Corinthians 10:31 "Do all for God's glory"

CHAPTER SEVEN

MAKING RIGHT CHOICES

Don't copy the behavior and customs of this world, but let God transform you into a new person by changing the way you think. Then you will learn to know God's will for you, which is good and pleasing and perfect. —ROMANS 12:2

Wouldn't it be great if all of our decisions were good, pleasing, and perfect in God's eyes and in keeping with His will for our lives?

The Bible tells us that if we allow God to transform us and change the way we think, then we can begin to make choices that Scripture describes as good, pleasing, and perfect. What a wonderful goal for all Christians particularly during trying times. Notwithstanding that God is at work within us to accomplish His purposes, the sad truth is that many of life's hardships are brought about by our own foolish or bad choices.

The lifelong process of transformation and growing as a follower of Christ should be a priority. Positive growth results in changing the way we think so that we are able to make godly decisions. This begs the question: How does God change the way we think?

For years, even though I grew up in a Christian family and attended church regularly, I had a blind spot in recognizing the relevance of the Bible to what I considered to be the real world. My thinking and decision-making therefore followed the world's pattern. This shouldn't have been a surprise as I seldom spent time in the Bible. Sunday mornings were my only exposure to God's Word. As a youth, I made a sincere and genuine profession of my faith in Jesus Christ, however, as an adult, I focused on pursuing the American Dream of success and I did so apart from God. God and the Bible were very neatly compartmentalized behind church doors.

This viewpoint continued until later in my life when my wife and I were invited to join a home Bible study led by an older couple with many years of experience helping others grow in their Christian faith. I reluctantly agreed to participate in what was supposed to last for only a few weeks; it continued for five years. With their patience, love, and encouragement with much prayer, I learned how to study the Bible and, most importantly, how to apply it to my life outside the walls of the church. It was then that the "changing the way you think" of Romans 12:2 began to occur and God began His transforming work which is still underway.

Much of God's Word focuses on behavior that is wise and pleasing to God. Making those right behavioral choices, however, can be clouded by a number of influences. What may look acceptable on the surface may in fact be the worst possible idea. There are times when decisions include actions or sacrifices that are contrary to the world's values or teaching. Unfortunately, many act according to the world's standards versus God's. Some rationalize their choice to move forward with questionable actions by justifying that the end result will benefit God. Ungodly means never justify perceived godly results! God is concerned as much about the when and how as He is with the end result.

While Scripture contains many specific commands and

direct statements that provide guidance, many decisions and choices are not explicitly covered. In such cases, the following guidelines can be helpful in evaluating courses of action and earnestly seeking God's best which always is good, pleasing, and perfect.

First and foremost, determine whether the action or choice is contrary to Scripture.

All Scripture is inspired by God and profitable for teaching, for reproof, for correction, for training in righteousness; so that the man of God may be adequate, equipped for every good work.

2 TIMOTHY 3:16-17 NASB

Any decision counter to Scripture should be avoided. Do not attempt to shape or redefine God's Word so as to allow you to do what you want. Implicit in this guideline is the necessity to know God's Word. How can you honor God, absent an awareness of His commands and principles? Seek godly counsel.

Ask God to search your heart.

Allow God to bring to your mind why you want to do this. Check your motives. Be honest with yourself. Search your heart and see if there are ungodly reasons (recognition, status, ego fulfillment, pride, or some other worldly mandate) tempting you to make a decision. You do have a choice. Don't be pressured into a decision without first seeking God's guidance.

Are physical and emotional conditions inhibiting your ability to make the right choice?

1 Kings 19 describes Elijah who was physically, mentally, and emotionally incapable of assessing his situation to make reasonable decisions. God's angel appeared and ordered him to sleep and eat in order to restore his senses and a proper perspective. Our current culture causes individuals to function

on the edge of exhaustion. God's advice may be to slow down, get needed nutrition, sleep and rest, and be restored and rejuvenated physically and mentally before acting. It's surprising how much your perspective changes with proper rest and taking a break away from the choice.

Will this choice become a burden?

Hebrews 12 portrays the Christian life as a race and tells us, "Let us lay aside every weight."

- Will I be so weighed down that I stop spending time in God's Word?
- Will it impact my spiritual growth?
- Will I be able to continue serving God?
- Will I no longer be available to God?
- Will the additional stress impact my personality and relationships?
- Will it prevent me from some valuable spiritual training?
- Will this lead to enslavement?

> *All things are lawful for me, but not all things are profitable...I will not be mastered.*
> 1 CORINTHIANS 6:12 NASB

A particular choice or behavior may not be sin, but it could lead to a form of enslavement through financial bondage, unbiblical relationships, unequal partnerships, or agreements with questionable parties.

Be aware of the following:

- It's possible to become addicted to anything (cars, TV, sports, exercise, and even all-consuming church activities that may be good but can be turned into substitutes for spending personal time with God via his Word and prayer). The most subtle forms of addiction are those things that on the surface appear good and inviting.

- Avoid or temper those situations that may lead to addiction.
- Do not allow materialism to enslave you to debt.
- Do not allow a choice to inhibit your being available for God's calling.

Will this decision be a stumbling stone to others?

> *All things are lawful for me, but may not be profitable.* —1 CORINTHIANS 6:12 NASB
>
> *Conduct yourself with wisdom toward outsiders, making the most of the opportunity.*
> —COLOSSIANS 4:5 NASB

Contrary to what some believe about the Christian faith being so rule-bound, we actually have much freedom. However, while many choices or actions may be permissible, they may not be profitable in terms of their negative influence upon others. The world watches Christians and, whether right or wrong, judges their actions and decisions based upon their opinion of what a "Christian" looks like and how they should behave. One of the biggest deterrents of the Christian faith is the world's perceived hypocrisy seen in those who claim to be followers of Christ.

Freedom is not a license to indulge or participate in anything that may negatively affect your relationships to and with non-Christians and thus impair their openness and coming to Christ. Disregarding appearance exhibits self-centeredness.

Guidelines:

- Behavior and choices should be an attraction to the Christian faith.

- If you are a complainer, have a critical spirit, have a questionable work product, exhibit a bad attitude, or continually have a "What's in it for me" approach to life—you will NOT be a positive influence.

- Shoddy work performance makes for a shoddy witness. Christians ought to be model employees. The choices you make at the workplace make a difference.

- Avoid actions that may be viewed negatively or put you in situations that impair or destroys your effectiveness as a Christlike example.

Will your decision honor God?

1 Corinthians 10:31 reminds us, *Whatever you do, do all to the glory of God.*

Will the results of your decision bring honor and glory to God?

As a result of your decision, could Jesus say to you, "Well done my good and faithful servant"?

Will this impact your church and service within the body of Christ?

- How often have we seen folks who are seemingly alive with Christ, serving in the church, holding key positions, devoting time in ministry suddenly drop out of the church's sight once they have taken a new job, work assignment, or recreation hobby?

- Will this contradict or be in line with your priorities?

- Keep in mind that "busyness" is the enemy of serving Christ and His church.

How will this impact your family? (It is important to include your spouse in this discussion.)

- Will this impact your spiritual role in your family?

- Will this make you an absentee spouse or parent?
- How will this impact your marriage and time with the children?
- What changes will this make in your family life?
- Will this change so fatigue and exhaust you that your family and God receive your second best and leftover effort?
- In addition to the above, if the decision is work-related:
  » Will you be able to leave your work at the office or will this consume all your time while at home?
  » Will there be additional travel demands required or excessive evening functions and weekends away from home?
  » Is money the primary factor making this choice appealing to you? Increasing your income can be good for your family and enable you to provide additional support for God's work—however, never at the expense of sacrificing your marriage or family. Don't be deceived and sacrifice your time with your spouse and children under the guise of "I'm doing it all for them!" Beware: In our culture, money, status, and materialism have become idols.
  » Could this decision turn you into a successful failure: successful in the world's eyes, but a failure in God's eyes.
  » Will this decision be based upon God's or the world's values?
  » In most cases, a wife needs her husband's love and attention; a husband needs his wife's respect. Make sure your decisions do not negatively impact either.

Seek the advice and counsel of godly men/women.

God has four primary ways of communicating to His children:

- Through His Word
- Through His Holy Spirit
- Through circumstances
- Through other believers

Seeking godly counsel can be helpful in thinking through decisions. Avoid shopping for counselors who are like-minded and tend to commiserate and agree with you, only telling you what you want to hear. That's not counsel; it's simply a license to do what you want.

When approaching a godly counselor avoid those who have a vested interest in your decision. It's unfair to them and may influence objectivity and create awkwardness. Failure to respect this may also create additional problems and damage the relationship as you realize their lack of objectivity and are forced to ignore their counsel.

When approaching one for counsel, be aware that you are seeking questions to ask yourself and/or helpful topics to help you think through the ramifications and implications of decisions. You are not asking the counselor to make the decision for you. Avoid asking the counselor, "What would you do?" This is irrelevant and a sign of failure to take responsibility. In addition, the counselor is not in your position or subject to the many factors that may be at work in your life or from God.

What does your common sense tell you to do?

God gave you a mind and expects you to use it. In Titus 2:12, we are commanded to "live soberly and righteously and godly in this present world" (ASV). The Greek word for "soberly" means sound-minded: sensible as opposed to foolish. This includes exercising good judgment and godly wisdom in such matters as relationships, priorities, values, financial management, acting responsibly with integrity, following good rules for health, practicing the disciplines of good mental and emotional intake, and living a balanced life.

Caution: *"The heart is deceitful above all things."*
—JEREMIAH 17:9 ASV

Common sense is all too often the "world's sense" which functions with significantly different values and priorities. Common sense can become deceived by the lure of the world's perceived fruits and lead to unwise decisions. It is highly recommended that you do not follow common sense separate from other guidelines; together, they are a good check and balance to decision making.

Note one important caveat: God can lead in a direction or action that appears to be foolish from the world's criteria. Scripture is full of such examples. Common sense in this listing applies to the normal and regular activities of our life, but we must always be open and receptive to God's special calling which may defy common sense.

Do you have peace about doing this? Why or why not?

Does everything appear to be positive, but you still do not have peace about your pending decision?

God's Holy Spirit resides in the lives of His children. Oftentimes, even after exploring all the guidelines and answering positively, one can still be burdened with anxiety. This may be God's intervention and the Holy Spirit speaking to you about this decision. Be attuned to that "still, small voice."

Are you getting ahead of God and not trusting in Him?

Wait for the Lord; be strong, and let your heart
take courage. Yes, wait for the Lord.

—PSALM 27:14 NASB

Oftentimes, we pray for God's intervention and His direction
about a decision of some perceived opportunity. However, in our
impatience, we quickly tire of waiting and act, rationalizing our
decision that God will intervene and stop or prevent such if it's
not his will. This belies our belief and prayers of seeking God's
guidance. Our quick acting is presumption. We are impatient
servants.

Only a fool goes through life acting independently from God.
Whose agenda are you following, God's or your own?

**What have you learned from your past experiences that should
be applied to this decision?**

Scripture is filled with situations where God commanded
His children to erect memorials or monuments so "that you
will not forget." Remembering who God is and what He has
done is important. Recall those times in your life that deserve
remembering. Likewise, quite often, the best teachers for
making good decisions are the unpleasant results of having
made bad decisions in the past. Examine your life experiences,
both good and bad, and evaluate your decisions and what you
learned to either apply or avoid.

What do you believe God wants you to do?

Decisions and choices should not be made in a vacuum apart
from prayer and seeking God's direction. When faced with a
decision, as God's children, our default position should be to
turn to our heavenly Father. Admittedly, there are those unique
situations when time doesn't allow pursuing the guidelines as
outlined above. This only underscores the importance of the
daily discipline of spending time in private reading God's Word
and in prayer.

Be sensitive to how certain verses or Biblical principles apply in your situation. It's a fact that the more time you spend with someone, the more you know them, their likes, dislikes, ways, and desires. It's the same with God. Our lives should be characterized by growing in communion with Him. As we grow, we become more discerning about His direction in making right decisions.

What a mistake it is for those who fail in this regard and seemingly live lives independently from God. Yet when faced with key decisions, run to and plead for His will and direction. God cares about every aspect of our lives and should not be relegated for only those perceived big decisions.

The good news is that it is never too late to begin to grow in a relationship wherein increasingly decisions are "good, pleasing, and perfect" (Romans 12:2).

A Disciple's Decision-Making Checklist

Scripture gives several characteristics of a disciple, a follower of Jesus Christ. These also can serve as decision-making criteria. If any option under consideration inhibits these characteristics, then it should be avoided. God will not honor any choice that violates what the Bible describes as a faithful follower of Christ.

Characteristics of a Disciple

✓ Honors God by doing whatever is on God's heart and mind. (I Samuel 2:35)

Does this decision bring honor to God?

✓ Glorifies God. (1 Corinthians 10:31; Colossians 3:17)

Does this decision glorify God?

✓ Embodies integrity. (Genesis 6:9)

Does this decision impact the integrity of my Christian witness to others?

✓ Embraces truth. (Ephesians 4:25)

Is this decision made based upon truth?

✓ Does things God's ways. (Isaiah 55:8-9; Psalms 25:4; 27:11)

Does this choice reflect man's or God's ways?

✓ Is trustworthy, honest, and faultless. (1 Thessalonians 2:10)

Is this decision honest and fair?

✓ Demonstrates wisdom. (Matthew 7:24-27)

Does this decision reflect the wisdom of the Bible?

✓ Abides, holds fast, obeys, and lives in accordance with God's Word. (John 8:31)

Does this decision adhere to God's Word?

✓ Exhibits unselfish love. (John 13:34-35; Matthew 22:37-39)

Does this decision serve others or myself?

✓ Has a high degree of commitment. (Matthew 10:37-39)

Does this decision impact godly priorities and commitments?

✓ Exercises spiritual gift(s). (1 Timothy 4:14)

Is this decision made after seeking the counsel of gifted others?

✓ Bears much fruit. (John 15:5, 8)

Will this decision impact my fruit-bearing going forward?

✓ Plays a role in the Great Commission. (Matthew 28:19-20) Will this decision impact my role in fulfilling the Great Commission?

✓ Serves as Christ's ambassador. (2 Corinthians 5:20)

Will this decision correctly represent Christ?

Chapter 7: Making Right Choices

Summary Points for Reflection

1. Many of life's hardships are brought about by our own foolish or bad choices.

2. God is at work within us to accomplish His purpose to make us more godly and Christlike. This applies to our choices and decisions.

3. The lifelong process of growing as a follower of Christ should be a priority. Positive growth results in changing the way we think so that we are able to make decisions that Scripture describes as good, pleasing, and perfect.

4. If we are to make choices that are pleasing to God, then it follows that we must know what pleases Him. God reveals this throughout His Word to us, the Bible.

5. The Bible is explicit in providing direction for many of life's decisions; however, there are many not specifically addressed. For these, the primary focus is not on the actual actions but rather on the probable results. Helpful guidelines consistent with Scripture are provided to assist making right choices.

Chapter 7: Questions for Meditation & Discussion

1. When facing a decision or choice, describe the process you typically use to decide your action.

2. Describe a difficult decision that you made in the past that was either "right" or "wrong" and explain why. What could have been done differently in your decision-making process?

3. What can you do to enable you to make right decisions in the future?

CHAPTER EIGHT

WHAT'S REALLY GOING ON? THE TRUTH!

A *pollo 13* ranks high on my list of all-time great movies. The story and suspense surrounding the safe return of the spaceship when faced with what appeared to be a disastrous and hopeless situation vividly illustrated the importance of perspective.

My favorite scene in this movie is the exchange between NASA Flight Director Gene Kranz and the mission control officer who after examining the situation, commented that all was lost and to prepare for damage control. Kranz saw the situation quite differently and immediately responded, "With all due respect sir, I believe this will be our finest hour." Work followed that delivered Apollo 13 safely home.

When hardship arrives we react. Our emotions may run high and at such times we need to examine the situation from a different perspective, one that provides insight, encouragement, and strength to endure.

Jesus tells us that He is "the way, the truth, and the life" (John 14:6). Whenever He refers to Himself with one of these words, the context is rich in meaning. Jesus is proclaiming that no one comes to God the Father except through Him. He is the only true way for one to be reconciled with and have a relationship with God. All other ways are false.

There is another aspect of Jesus being the truth that is related to God's perspective on circumstances and situations. We are finite; we look at a situation and draw conclusions from what we observe or know, and then make an interpretation of how we define the truth of that circumstance. The Gospels however are full of situations where man's perspective of truth was very different from that of Jesus.

If you were to ask the disciples in the midst of the life-threatening storm at sea what was true, no doubt, they would tell you the truth was they were going to drown! Their view of the truth was that Jesus didn't care for them; He was fast asleep while they were frantically trying to survive. On the other hand, if one were to ask Jesus what was true, He would have explained how this adversity was a test of the disciples' faith and an opportunity to display His divine power over nature by quieting the sea. Jesus' first response upon calming the sea was, "Where's your faith?"

Another example is found in the situation of Mary and Martha's anxiety over the death of Lazarus and Jesus' delay in coming. We again see two different versions of truth. If you were to ask the sisters in the midst of their grief what was truth, most likely they would tell you that the truth was that Lazarus died only because Jesus lingered and did not arrive in time to save their brother. Jesus revealed later, however, that the real truth of this situation was that Lazurus died so that He could make a significant revelation of His deity; He could raise the dead and declare victory over death.

We also see this error as exhibited by two of Jesus' followers who were journeying to another town following the crucifixion. In Luke 24:13-32, we read that the unrecognizable, resurrected Jesus appeared alongside these two men. As they walked, they described to Jesus the events that had taken place regarding Jesus' crucifixion. Their description of the events to Jesus was truth as they interpreted it. They even went so far as to say, "We had hoped He was the Messiah who had come to rescue Israel." Their version of truth was that Jesus was nothing more than a good teacher and prophet but not God's Messiah. Jesus had disappointed them and not performed as they expected. They interpreted truth and characterized Jesus as a failure.

Again in John 9:1-3 we see Jesus' perspective of reality and truth, which clearly differed from the disciples: "As he went along, he saw a man blind from birth. His disciples asked him, 'Rabbi, who sinned, this man or his parents, that he was born blind?' 'Neither this man nor his parents sinned,' said Jesus, 'but this happened so that the works of God might be displayed in him'" (NIV). The disciples mistakenly viewed the cause or purpose of this hardship. Jesus corrected them by informing them of God's view. The truth of this situation had nothing to do with sin, but existed in order to bring honor to God by displaying His power.

Repeatedly, throughout the Gospels, we see the real truth of God's purpose. The lesson is that man views the truth of life's situations, trials, and hardships only at surface level. God sees things quite differently. He is truth and is active and ever-present in the lives of His children. By His Holy Spirit residing in us, God will guide and help us see His truth in our times of trial. At such times, we need to pray and be in God's Word asking him to open our eyes to His truth, perspective, and understanding of what He's doing through each of life's trying circumstances.

There are those times of crisis when everything around us seems lost and overwhelming. During such times, we may be prone to view our situation as the world sees it: hopeless. Contrary to such thinking, God is active, ever-present, and very much in control.

We can learn and be encouraged by a situation as described in 2 Kings 6:15-18. The king of Aram launched his army with a mission of killing Elisha whom the king considered a traitor. Aram sent a great army of many troops, horses, and chariots to the city hosting Elisha. The king's orders were to kill him and all his servants and followers.

Scripture describes this experience, "When the servant of the man of God got up early the next morning and went outside, there were troops, horses and chariots everywhere. 'Oh, sir, what will we do now?' the young man cried to Elisha. 'Don't be afraid!' Elisha told him. 'For there are more on our side than on theirs!' Then Elisha prayed, 'O Lord open his eyes and let him see!' The Lord opened the young man's eyes, and when he looked up, he saw the hillside around Elisha was filled with horses and chariots of fire. As the Aramean army advanced toward him, Elisha prayed, 'O Lord please make them blind.' So the Lord struck them with blindness as Elisha asked." The story continues that Elisha caused them to be led away to a distant city and then asked that their eyes be opened; they were fed; and they returned home.

There are those times in our lives when we need to pray like Elisha, "O God, open my eyes and let me see!" Our version of truth is all too often based on what we earthly see. We may not be aware of God's "horses and chariots of fire" that He provides around us. God never leaves us alone to face life's trials and adversities; He is always with us to provide deliverance or the strength to endure. Often, the truth of the crisis is that God is able to display His power by giving visible evidence of His work in a hurting world.

This need is echoed by Henry Blackaby in his book on *Spiritual Leadership*, "People see things from a temporal view. Spiritual leaders court disaster when they panic and assume they must take matters in their own hands. When spiritual leaders wait patiently on the Lord, regardless of how long it takes, God always proves himself absolutely true to His word."[21]

God's purpose may not be readily apparent or revealed as quickly as we would prefer. At such times God calls upon us to trust and have unwavering faith in Him. We see examples of this in the Scriptures. When Mary was informed that she was to give birth to the baby, Jesus, she didn't grasp the magnitude of God's intentions but Luke 2:19 does indicate that Mary was growing in her understanding, "but Mary kept all these things in her heart and thought about them often."

Mary also didn't understand many of Jesus' actions. His first recorded miracle in John 2 was at a wedding feast when He instructed the attendants to fill the empty wine jars with water. This perplexed the servants who came to Mary for some explanation. She had no answers or explanations other than simply telling them to obey, "Do whatever He tells you," (John 2:5). There may be times when we do not understand and need to heed Mary's instructions and simply be obedient and trust.

When we find ourselves like the panic-stricken disciples, the accusatory Mary and Martha, the questioning mother of Jesus, or the two discouraged followers on the road, we should never assume that our surface interpretation is true. During those times when God appears distant and unengaged in our situation, we can be assured that He is infinitely more reliable than our fickle emotions or conclusions.

Many of life's hardships may not be clear during this lifetime since God's ways are so much higher than ours; however, there will be a time when God's goodness and purposes will become clear. First Corinthians 13:12 reminds us, "Now we see things imperfectly, like puzzling reflections in a mirror, but then we will see everything with perfect clarity. All that I know now is partial and incomplete, but then I will know everything completely, just as God now knows me completely." A close Christian friend told me that he expects one of the first things we'll say when in heaven, when all things become clear and understandable is, "But of course."

The truth of any circumstance or situation is God's view of reality and not ours. With God, when nothing is happening, something is always happening.

Chapter 8: What's Going On? The Truth!

Summary Points for Reflection

1. Our natural response is to panic and take matters in our own hands during times of crisis.

2. When hardship strikes and emotions peak, we need to stop, gain control of ourselves, and examine the situation from a different perspective that provides insight, encouragement, and strength to endure.

3. Our version of the truth of life's hardships is all too often based on what we earthly see.

4. The truth of any circumstance or situation is God's view of reality and not ours.

5. God's unchanging mission is to bring honor and glory to Himself and to restore the broken relationship with sinful man. Life's hardships must be viewed from the perspective of how each one complements God's purposes.

6. There may be times when we do not understand and need to be obedient and trust in our loving Father God.

Chapter 8: Questions for Meditation & Discussion

1. Think of a time in your life when you looked upon a situation in one way and later saw it differently. What did you learn from this experience?

2. Review the experience of Mary and Martha in John 11:1-44 as they were waiting on Jesus to come to their brother's aid. Have you ever been in a situation where you experienced such anxiety and emotions along with disappointment in God? Describe.

3. What assurance and hope can we find in the following verses:

> Isaiah 55:8-9
>
> 1 Corinthians 13:12?
>
> John 13:7

4. What can you do to prevent seeing events and experiences from man's perspective and grow in your ability to recognize what is "true" from God's perspective?

CHAPTER NINE

DOES PRAYER WORK?

D oes prayer really work?

In Mark Twain's classic, *Adventures of Huckleberry Finn*, Huck gave the whole matter of prayer much thought and came to a conclusion shared by many well-meaning Christians:

Miss Watson she took me in the closet and prayed, but nothing come of it. She told me to pray every day, and whatever I asked for I would get it. But it warn't so. I tried it. Once I got a fish-line, but no hooks. It warn't any good to me without hooks. I tried for the hooks three or four times, but somehow I couldn't make it work. By and by, one day, I asked Miss Watson to try for me, but she said I was a fool. She never told me why, and I couldn't make it out no way.

I set down one time back in the woods, and had a long think about it. I says to myself, if a body can get anything they pray for, why don't Deacon Winn get back the money he lost on pork? Why can't the widow get back her silver snuffbox that was stole? Why can't Miss Watson fat up? No, says I to myself, there ain't nothing in it. I went and told the widow about it, and she said the thing a body could get by praying for it was spiritual gifts. This was too many for me, but she told me what she meant—I must help other people, and do everything I could for other people, and look out for them all the time, and never think about myself. This was including Miss Watson, as I took it. I went out in the woods and turned it over in my mind a long time, but I couldn't see no advantage about it—except for the other people; so at last I reckoned I wouldn't worry about it anymore, but just let it go."[22]

Unfortunately, Huck's not alone today. Far too many Christians just "let it go" after coming to God in prayer asking Him to sign their blank check or deliver their grocery list for whatever they desire or need, all the while expecting Him to perform.

Where does this line of thinking come from? No doubt, most will agree that it is not Biblical to pray for God to grant our every wish and desire. On the one hand, we say with confidence that it is wrong to pray for certain things, while on the other, it is right and Biblical to pray for others. What makes the difference? We need to examine Scriptures that provide insight into prayers that seemingly give Christians both a blank check as well as the assurance that God will act according to our every request.

You don't have to search long for examples that seem to offer this benefit to God's children. For example:

If you remain in Me and My words remain in you, you may ask for anything you want, and it will be granted. —JOHN 15:7

Ask, using My name, and you will receive, and you will have abundant joy. —JOHN 16:24

Keep on asking and you will receive what you ask for ... for everyone who asks, receives.
—MATTHEW 7:7-8

And we are confident that He hears us whenever
we ask for anything that pleases Him. And since
He hears us when we make our requests, we also
know that He will give us what we ask for.

—1 JOHN 5:14-15

Jesus' parable in Luke 18:1-8 of the persistent widow is explained by Jesus in the opening verse, "One day Jesus told His disciples a story to show that they should always pray and never give up."

Admittedly, there is much about prayer that we do not fully understand. Each of these verses becomes problematic if we interpret them to mean God is at our disposal to grant our every wish by simply asking. Experience contradicts such a belief. Without question, God certainly can and does grant many specific requests; however, there are just as many times when prayers and requests seem unanswered.

Unanswered prayers can create confusion or even doubt. This is particularly true during times of hardship. Based upon how we interpret certain Bible verses regarding prayer, questions may arise when God doesn't act as requested. When this happens, some may conclude that God doesn't listen or they react to unfilled requests by questioning the integrity and credibility of Scripture.

Sadly, there may be those who believe this is a reflection of their perceived lack of faith or some misguided feeling that they have to earn God's favor in order to have their prayers answered. As I painfully experienced in my own life, these views are grossly in error.

Many years ago, I was meeting with a young man through a series of Bible studies. As our relationship grew, I learned that his family's background was filled with many unbiblical beliefs. One in particular was that if you make a continuous request to God, and believed hard enough with faith, then God will perform.

Over time, I learned things were not well at home and his marital problems were increasing in severity. It wasn't long before his marriage dissolved and his wife filed for divorce despite our prayers and his pleadings.

The very thought of divorce was unimaginable to my friend. He refused to accept the reality of the situation and repeatedly claimed that God would never allow this to happen to him, a Christian. He was convinced that this crisis would be resolved by God's intervention. He prayed continuously claiming that his marriage would be restored. During divorce proceedings, he proudly announced to the court that nothing they did or said would make any difference because God was not going to allow a divorce to be granted. Sadly, his sincere, but errant positive confession and belief failed. The divorce was granted.

My friend was devastated. To him, either he had failed to have enough faith or God had failed to honor his belief and prayer requests. Either of these options crushed his Christian faith. This coupled with the pain of losing his family was traumatic.

A few days later, I received a call informing me that his body was discovered in his car on a lonely country road slumped in the driver's seat with a revolver still clasped in his hands! Tragic! What a victory for the adversary, Satan!

Prayer Promises

What then are the promises about God answering our prayers as contained in the verses mentioned earlier? The answers are found by examining each verse in its context without overlooking phrases that are included such as "if you remain in Me," "using My name," and "ask for anything that pleases Him." These create an added dimension and condition to prayers. They include the assumption and expectation that we will have such an intimate abiding relationship with our Father God that our requests will be in line with His will and pleasure, not necessarily ours. As such, He will grant our requests. When viewed from this perspective, verses like John 14:13 that include the promise, "Whatever you ask in My name, that will I do that the Father may be glorified in the Son" (NASB) are better understood.

Allow me to offer a personal illustration that may help in understanding.

When I was the CEO of a large corporation, I had several assistants and senior officers reporting to me. We spent a great deal of time together and soon they began to know what I did and didn't like; what I would approve and disapprove; and what I expected. They knew that some actions or requests were fine and they felt comfortable acting on my behalf or bringing them to me. However, they also knew that some proposals or actions would be contrary to what I wanted and they never brought these to my attention. There were also times when they used my name and authority in getting things done. They knew this was permissible since they would only do things that pleased me and were consistent with what they knew I wanted. They respected my authority and accepted what I said because they trusted me and understood that I would only do what I believed to be best for them and the company. There were also times when I approved their requests apart from the company's mission and based more upon our relationship. It gave me pleasure in giving them what they wanted up to a point of not threatening the organization or against their best interests.

In many respects, this business example has spiritual applications. The closer we are to God, and the more intimately we know Him, then the more in line are our prayer requests with His mission, will, desires, and His work of transformation in our lives. When this happens, we can be confident that He will respond and give us what we ask. We also must develop the trust in Him to know that when our specific prayer requests go unanswered, He knows best. He wants only His good for us and His timetable and much grander purposes may be different than ours. He may see our needs and wants in a very different way, and He may have something entirely different for us than we are aware.

God's ways are far different from those of man. God may have a far greater mission and purpose for not granting our requests. Many of our prayers focus entirely on what we want versus what He may want or be orchestrating for His purpose. The closer we walk with God and spend time in His Word, the nature of our requests begins to conform more to His agenda rather than our own.

With all this in mind, have you ever listened to yourself praying?

Most of us tend to ramble, repeat ourselves, and treat God as if He doesn't know what's going on or has been asleep or absent and needs to be caught up on what's happening. There are also those times in well-meaning Christian circles when it is unclear if praying is speaking to God or using "prayer" as a means of informing others of all the details of a situation. Some pastors use prayer as another mode of preaching to highlight or summarize their message versus coming before God with their requests. I find myself thinking, "Is he talking to us or to God?"

I'm reminded of my young grandson and our conversations. Most of these are his telling me all about his day and the things he's excited about and wants me to know. For the most part, he includes everything that he wants me to do and where he wants me to take him. I love hearing him talk and seeing his excitement and his unique expressions. I dearly love him. I typically have to interrupt to get any words in, and most often he simply ignores what I'm telling him, as what he has to say is far more important in his young mind.

I wonder if this might describe how we often communicate with God. Prayer too often becomes a monologue with us telling

God all about ourselves and going through our list of all the things we want Him to do, and then saying, "Amen." No doubt, God loves us and wants to hear all about us, but He also wants to say a few things to us. Unfortunately, and like my interaction with my grandson, we never give Him time. In our busy lives and hurried culture, we have lost the discipline of coming before God and listening to and for His still small "voice." We would do well to stop, look, come and listen, and "be still and know that I am God!"

We should be sensitive to what God wants to say to us. How many times when we read Scripture does a certain verse seem to jump out at us? We may even highlight or underline it and then unfortunately move on. Wait! Stop! We must not overlook that God's Holy Spirit residing in us may be getting our attention via that verse that has something in its meaning and application that God wants us to hear. Develop a seeking and discerning mind to discover God's voice whenever reading His Holy Word. If we fail to respond and "listen" for God via his Word, then He may resort to other means in our lives to get our attention.

As Jesus neared the last days of his earthly ministry and was preparing his disciples for his departure, He told them some profound truths regarding one of the roles of the Holy Spirit.

> *There is so much more I want to tell you, but you can't bear it now. When the Spirit of truth comes, He will guide you into all truth. He will not speak on His own but will tell you what He has heard. He will tell you about the future. He will bring me glory by telling you whatever He receives from Me. All that belongs to the Father is mine; this is why I said, 'The Spirit will tell you whatever He receives from Me.* —JOHN 16:12-15

This is an amazing truth. The Holy Spirit that lives in each of us as God's children will communicate with us personally everything that He receives from Jesus. Think about that. What do you suppose that Jesus wants to tell you? Allow me to suggest that it could focus on His transforming work in making us more godly and Christlike, or possibly some assignment He wants us to perform in line with His mission to bring Him glory.

All of this comes within the process of growing in our knowing God and cultivating a deep and intimate loving relationship with Him. We must cultivate the discipline to regularly spend time with Him in His Word prayerfully reading, meditating, listening, and seeking that still, small voice as He reveals Himself and His will. This builds a firm foundation for when adversity strikes. Without this, as Jesus said in describing those who don't build their lives on strong spiritual foundations, when hardship comes, they *"collapse with a mighty crash!"* (Matthew 7:24-27).

The Bible's Prayers

We gain further insight into God's purposes and what is on His heart by closely examining prayers in the Bible. Look closely at the Apostle Paul's many prayers in the Bible. They tend to be remarkably different from ours. It is noteworthy that during the direst circumstances, he prayed for endurance, boldness, thankfulness, confidence in witnessing, and for ways to use each situation as an opportunity to honor and bring glory to God. Paul was mindful of God's mission.

During times of adversity, we would do well to seek the attributes that Paul valued. His life was filled with adversity and what we would consider extreme hardship. Most of his letters were written while he was imprisoned. He was beaten until near dead, scorned by many, shipwrecked, snake bitten, and suffered affliction with an unnamed disease. Yet, he described these as "momentary light afflictions" (2 Corinthians 4:17 NASB) when compared to knowing God! One might expect his prayers to be filled with, "Lord, make them stop...heal these wounds...get me out of prison...punish these guys!" Paul's prayers continually focused on his mission for God and his desire to use every circumstance as an opportunity for boldness to witness for God and Christ's glory! Paul was focused and mission-minded in spite of the circumstance.

Having said all this, is it okay to make our specific requests to God? Does God want to hear our heart's desires? Yes, and again, yes! We are encouraged to make our requests known to Him, and He does grant many of our specific prayers. However, as we grow in knowing God, there is a subtle change in our asking as we mature and our requests come more in line with the things that are important to Him.

Back to my illustration of parents and children, how often have you heard a parent talk about how much their relationship with their children has changed and deepened over time? It's not unusual for a mom or dad to comment how enjoyable and more adult their conversations have become as their child has matured. This may also be true for us with our Father God as we grow in our relationship.

God can and often does grant the desires of our heart. Scripture is filled with examples where God delivered people from their hardship, as well as many who were strengthened through their circumstances. Whichever, we need to develop the faith of Shadrach, Meshach, and Abednego as shown in Daniel 3:17-18. Their response to the evil king when standing at the doorway of the fiery furnace is noteworthy, "Our God is able to deliver us from this furnace of blazing fire and He will deliver us out of your hand, O king; but even if He does not, we are not going to serve your gods or idols." We must never forget the "but even if He does not" in our prayer relationship with our loving Father. In the midst of crisis and hardship, our God is able to deliver us; but even if He does not, we will continue to trust Him and seek His purposes and strength to endure and honor Him.

During times of adversity when our prayers for deliverance go unanswered, 1 Corinthians 10:13 contains a reassuring promise of help and strength. "The temptations in your life are no different from what others experience. And God is faithful. He will not allow the temptation to be more than you can stand. When you are tempted, He will show you a way out so that you can endure."

Four noteworthy truths are found in this Scriptural promise:

1. Even though you might believe your pain and crisis situation is unique—it's not. Others have experienced similar or far worse circumstances.

2. God is faithful. He never deserts His children, and even though you may not sense His presence, He is there and knows exactly what's happening and what you're feeling; He hears and understands your prayers, and knows the purpose and results of your trial.

3. He will show you His way and what to do during this time of adversity. He may or may not expect you to take some form of action as much as He desires you to come closer to Him.

4. He will provide sufficient grace and supernatural strength to endure. His answer may be contrary to your prayer for quick deliverance as His desire may be to endure in a manner that brings honor and glory to Him and others around you.

As noted above, this perspective respects the fact that God's ways and thoughts and desires are much higher than ours as attested in Isaiah 55:8-9, "'My thoughts are nothing like your thoughts,' says the Lord. 'And, My ways are far beyond anything you could imagine. For just as the heavens are higher than the earth, so My ways are higher than your ways and My thoughts higher than your thoughts.'" Our prayers should express the desires of our hearts, but ought to acknowledge and seek His higher ways and thoughts.

Our "Big" God

We must never discount to whom we are speaking when praying. Our prayers during times of trials are directly related to our beliefs about God. The more we grow in knowing Him and the "bigger" He is to us, then the "smaller" is our view of life's challenging trials. Theologian J.B. Phillips challenges us with his exhortation, "Your God is too small!"[23] This reminds us that we have a "big" and great God who loves us and is with us at all times to care for us. Accepting this changes how we react to life's adversities. If our knowledge of God is sparse and "small," then we are prone to allow the impact of our situations to become "bigger" than Him. We can find comfort in knowing that no crisis is too big for God to handle with His enabling presence and provision of supernatural strength. We serve a "big" and great God.

God has wonderful plans for us, His children, that dwarf any of this world's problems or hardships. 1 Corinthians 2:9 reminds us that, "No eye has seen, no ear has heard, and no mind has imagined what God has prepared for those that love Him." And, Jeremiah 29:11-14 gives us wonderful insight into God's presence and desires, "'For I know the plans I have for you,' says the Lord. 'They are plans for good and not for disaster, to give you a future and a hope. In those days when you pray, I will listen. If you look for Me wholeheartedly, you will find Me. I will be found by you, says the Lord.'"

Isaiah 40:28-31 speaks of how big and powerful our God is, "Have you never heard? Have you never understood? The Lord is the everlasting God, the Creator of all the earth. He never grows weak or weary. No one can measure the depths of his understanding. He gives power to the weak and strength to the powerless. Even youths will become weak and tired, and young men will fall in exhaustion. But those who trust in the Lord will find new strength. They will soar high on wings like eagles. They will run and not grow weary. They will walk and not faint." God is our loving heavenly Father. In this role, He loves us far beyond what we can ever realize. His love is vast and incredible; the Creator and only true and living God loves us! He loves us so much that He sacrificed His Son just to have a relationship with each one of us—YOU! Think about that!

This love opens His heart to listen to every request and He understands our every emotion and desire. He delights in granting requests that in His divine knowledge He knows will be best. However, as a loving Father, He wants His children to grow in godliness and conformity to His Son, Jesus, and He desires for a lost world to be reconciled and restored to Himself. We should always keep this in mind and ask God to open our eyes and give us discerning minds to recognize His path and desires.

With His love and mission in perfect balance, He will answer every prayer. His answers may not be as we ask or in the time frame we expect, but God does hear and respond to the prayers of His children. It is we who often fail to recognize or accept His answers.

Jesus and Prayer

One cannot read of Jesus' earthly ministry without noting that one of his chief characteristics was the importance of prayer and His being continually in touch with His Father God. Jesus' life reflected a commitment to prayer seldom seen in most believers' lives. This was true to the end as He prayed all that night in the garden and then later while dying on the cross. Throughout the Gospels, Jesus is seen withdrawing from the crowds or rising early to spend time in prayer.

In Luke 22:42, we see Jesus subjecting even Himself to His Father God's will in His garden prayer before His impending death by crucifixion, "Father, if You are willing, please take this cup of suffering away from me. Yet I want your will to be done, not mine." And, Hebrews 5:7-8 references this by telling us that, "While Jesus was here on earth, He offered prayers and pleadings with a loud cry and tears to the one who could rescue Him from death. And, God heard his prayers because of His deep reverence for God. Even though Jesus was God's Son, He learned obedience from the things He suffered."

Note the truths as included in these two verses:

- Jesus acknowledged God as His loving Father
- Jesus acknowledged God as having the power to rescue Him and do anything
- Jesus made His specific request for deliverance
- Jesus subjected Himself to God's will
- Jesus knew God was able to rescue Him
- God heard His prayer
- Jesus learned obedience from suffering

We need look no farther than Jesus, who endured the humiliation, pain, and suffering leading up to the cross and His public death. He prayed for an alternative but submitted to God. God answered His prayers by providing the strength to endure that which would bring salvation to a lost world. God could have rescued Jesus, but then God's mission would be violated. God achieved a far greater result by not answering Jesus' heartfelt request.

There are those times when God doesn't expect us to understand but only to trust Him. Our faith is not based upon a Mr. Fix-It or a Genie-in-a-Bottle, but rather on a loving Father that seeks His best for us in accomplishing His mission and purpose via our growing maturity into Christlikeness.

Elisabeth Elliot, author and widow of slain missionary Jim Elliot, reflected on the importance of displaying trust and faith during times of adversity:

> There is such a thing as obedient faith that does not depend on receiving only benefits. Jesus had to show the world that He loved the Father and would, no matter what happened, do exactly what He said. The servant is not greater than his Lord. When we cry, "Why, Lord?" we should more correctly ask instead, "Why not, Lord, shall I not follow my Master in suffering as in everything else?"
>
> Does our faith depend on having every prayer answered as we think it should be answered, or does it rest rather on the character of a sovereign Lord? We can't really tell, can we, until we're in real trouble. We must show the world what genuine faith is—the kind of faith that overcomes the world because it trusts and obeys, no matter what the circumstances. The world does not want to be told. The world must be shown. Isn't that part of the answer to the great question of why Christians suffer?[24]

The following principles will help us frame our perspective on the Bible's prayer promises:

1. God wants us to come to Him and honestly pour out our hearts and requests (Philippians 4:6-7). Even our Lord Jesus asked for deliverance from having to go to His death on the cross. However, in His submission to God's will, He added, "nevertheless, not My will but Yours." It's the "nevertheless" that we are prone to overlook.

2. God's primary and overriding theme and mission throughout the Bible is to bring honor and glory to Himself and to restore a broken relationship. Everything that happens must be viewed as it relates to God's mission. It follows that we need to examine our prayer requests to come in line with God's desires.

3. God's ways and thoughts are not like man's (Isaiah 55:8-9). Our view, thoughts, requests and desires are typically focused on self. God may have something totally different in mind.

4. The truth of any circumstance or situation is God's view of reality and not ours. We need to see the unseen and what God may be doing or how He might use each hardship to accomplish His purpose and mission.

5. Perceived unanswered prayer requests are not an indication of God's lack of love or His power to do whatever He so pleases. God always seeks our good and to accomplish His purposes.

6. There will be those times when we do not understand, but God wants us to trust in Him as our loving Father.

7. The closer and more intimate relationship we have with God in His Word, and the more we grow in knowing Him; then the more our prayers and requests come in line with His agenda versus our own.

8. We can be encouraged and challenged by Paul's exhortation in 1 Thessalonians 5:17-18, "Never stop praying. Be thankful in all circumstances, for this is God's will for you who belong to Christ Jesus."

Our Loving Father God

I learn much about trusting God and His loving response

to my prayers from my own experiences as a father and grandparent. I can recall taking our children to new places. As we approached these unfamiliar settings filled with strangers, they would immediately reach for my hand. They needed assurance that they were not alone; I would watch over them. When they would react or tell me they were afraid, I would always listen, comfort, and reassure them.

There were also those times when they courageously ventured out on their own but always periodically glancing at me across the room. Nothing was said; our eye contact was enough to let them know I was there. During one such visit, I had left the room for a short time only to return and find my four year old in a state of panic and crying. He felt alone and was terrified. No amount of comforting from strangers helped overcome his fear. He wanted his father who he knew loved him and would take care of him. When I reappeared, he ran to me and within minutes was at peace and all was well.

Like young children, there may be times when we find ourselves in dark, unfamiliar, and threatening situations. Feelings of loneliness and insecurity may overcome us. We can find comfort during such times in knowing that our loving Father God is always with us and will never leave us alone. We can run to Him in our prayers; He hears and is always there to reach out His hand and hold us to assure us of His presence. Nothing can ever separate us from His presence and love.

We may not understand or feel God's presence during times of hardship. It may be that the only thing that we can hold onto is His promise:

> *Can anything ever separate us from Christ's love?*
> *Does it mean He no longer loves us if we have*
> *trouble or calamity, or are persecuted, or hungry,*
> *or destitute, or in danger, or threatened with*
> *death? No, despite all these things, overwhelming*

*victory is ours through Christ, who loved us. And
I am convinced that nothing can ever separate us
from God's love. Neither death nor life, neither
angels nor demons, neither our fears for today
nor our worries about tomorrow—not even
the powers of hell can separate us from God's
love. No power in the sky above or in the earth
below—indeed, nothing in all creation will ever
be able to separate us from the love of God that
is revealed in Christ Jesus our Lord.*

—ROMANS 8:35-39

*The Lord is my Helper, I will not be seized with
alarm; I will not fear or dread or be terrified.*

—HEBREWS 13: AMPLIFIED

Chapter 9: Does Prayer Work?

Summary Points for Reflection

1. Far too many Christians treat God like one who exists to meet their every desire or perceived need. When God doesn't perform or deliver as expected, the results can be disappointment, disillusionment, disregard of God and the Bible and in extreme situations, devastating.

2. The Bible provides insight into prayers that seemingly give Christians a blank check as well as the assurance that God will act according to our every request. Many of the Bible's prayer promises are conditional.

3. God certainly wants His children to pour out their hearts and to bring their desires and requests to Him.

4. With God's love and mission in perfect balance, He will answer every prayer. Many times His answers will be as requested; however, there will be times when they will not be as asked or in the time frame expected.

5. God doesn't expect us to understand but instead to trust Him. Our faith is not based upon a Mr. Fix-It or a Genie-in-a-Bottle, but rather on a loving Father that seeks His best for us in accomplishing His mission and purpose via our growing maturity into Christlikeness.

6. Nothing can ever separate us from God's presence and love. The Bible assures us that He hears and responds to the prayers of His children. It is we who often fail to recognize or accept His answers.

Chapter 9: Questions for Meditation & Discussion

1. How would you describe your prayer life?

2. Prayer is often described as "communication with God." Examine a dictionary's definition of communication and apply the various definitions and descriptions to prayer with God.

3. What can you learn from the many recorded instances of Jesus' prayer life as noted in the Gospels?

4. What do the following verses teach about prayer?

> Hebrews 4:16
> 1 Thessalonians 5:16-18
> Colossians 4:2
> James 5:16

5. Prayers vary in content and purpose. Match the following verses with their respective purpose.

Hebrews 13:15	Specific Request
Colossians 1:3 and Ephesians 5:20	Praise
James 5:16	Intercession for others
Ephesians 6:18	Thanks
Luke 11:3	Confession

6. Read Luke 10:38-42 of Jesus visiting the sisters, Mary and Martha. Describe the actions of Mary and Martha during this time of Jesus' visit. How might this look today in the lives of Christians? Which of the two sisters' behavior best describes you?

7. How does knowing our mission of loving, honoring, and glorifying God impact our prayers? Explain.

8. Are your prayers typically a monologue? Perhaps it is time to let God "speak" to you through his Word. What steps can you take to revise and improve your personal prayer life?

CHAPTER TEN

GOD'S WORKSHOP AND CLASSROOM

Some years ago the acronym "PBPGINFWMY" was a popular bumper sticker that while humorous contained much truth. "Please Be Patient God Is Not Finished With Me Yet" reminds us that our lives are God's workshop as He shapes and transforms us into Christlikeness.

This training in godliness includes God's use of our experiences during times of hardship. They are tests and trials by which we learn to rely upon and apply the truths and promises of what He has proclaimed in His Word. These events draw us closer to God where we grow in knowing Him and His faithfulness. This is spiritual on-the-job training. French author, Madame Guyon (1648-1717), knew of such experiences when during a time of crisis she wrote, "I have learned to love the darkness of sorrow, for it is there that I best see the brightness of God's face."

The Apostle Paul comments on the value of knowing Christ in Philippians 3:8, "I consider everything a loss compared to the surpassing greatness of *knowing* Christ Jesus my Lord, for whose sake I have lost all things. I consider them rubbish that I may gain Christ" (NIV 18984). Jesus refers to knowing God in His prayer the night of His arrest in the garden leading to His death, "Now this is eternal life: that they may *know* You, the only true God, and Jesus Christ, whom You sent to earth" (John 17:3 NIV).

It's noteworthy that the Greek word as used in these verses for knowledge and knowing is *epignosis*. This is actually two Greek words which, when joined together, give an additional meaning. *Epi* is Greek for "intense." When attached to the customary Greek word for knowledge, *gnosis*, it communicates a much more intense form of knowledge than mere intellectual assent.

Typically this "knowing" comes through the experience of personally seeing or experiencing God at work. In this regard, it refers to an experiential knowledge. I can know something by reading it and intellectually believe it to be true. For example, I can read the label telling me that a small stepladder can hold my weight. However, when I climb up the ladder, I can then experientially know that it is true—that is *epignosis*, a much higher and more credible aspect of knowledge.

Similarly, does your faith grow the most from reading God's promises or when you actually relied upon Him and experienced His supernatural work in the midst of a personal trial? Both are important, and this is not to minimize the importance of time in God's Word. There is, however, a big difference in personally experiencing God's working in your life by trusting in and applying His Word versus reading of God's promises absent experience and application.

This truth was validated recently when I contacted several individuals whom I consider spiritually mature. I asked each a question: "Looking back at your life, what has been the biggest contributor to your spiritual growth?" No additional questions or directions were provided. Their answers included Bible study, Scripture memory, prayer, mission trips, and other memorable experiences or disciplines. However, without exception, each responded immediately that the number one contributor to their growth was a time of adversity. Each described a specific period during which he or she relied upon faith and trust in God and experienced seeing Him work. The common denominator for each was a time of desperation and need.

In many respects, our lives are God's classroom where He as our teacher shapes and molds us into Christlikeness via various growth experiences often disguised as hardships. Some lessons take time for us to learn and may involve repetition. We may even miss or ignore them. If we miss something or simply don't get it the first time, He may allow us to go through another trial until we do. It may not feel any better the second or third time, so it behooves us to pay attention to each time of testing. We need to be sensitive and discerning to discover the opportunity for growth that might result in times of hardship. God is always at work to bring us to Christlikeness. In this respect, life's many trials are purposeful.

Some trials are more subtle and may appear as periods of time when God is seemingly inactive. He may appear to be aloof and afar. This may create frustration and feelings of being in a desolate desert absent of purpose, direction, and a feeling of being ignored by Him. We've heard or perhaps even said ourselves, "I just don't sense God's presence and seem disconnected to Him."

Those desertlike times may be God's signal that He wants to spend extended time with you to renew and strengthen the relationship or reveal a task or greater assignment. During these times, it is important to retreat to a quiet place, preferably for a few days. Take your Bible and seek God in prayer and time in the Scripture. Allow Him to speak via His Word.

The desert is a classroom of silence and solitude. The English word "desert" comes from the Hebrew word *dahbaar* which means "to speak." It is a place where God may be silent or speak the loudest. Likewise, in the midst of isolation and barrenness, it provides an environment where the devil may speak. God used this setting to prepare Biblical leaders and teach lessons in godliness. Both Moses and Jesus spent time in the desert in preparation for the mission that awaited them.

Moses had to spend forty years in God's desert classroom in preparation for one of God's greatest assignments; Jesus spent forty days in the desert and was unyielding to the various categories of temptations He would face during His earthly ministry. Both of these times were preparatory in nature.

Moses failed his first test of obedience by taking matters into his own hands and killing an Egyptian taskmaster (Exodus 2:13-15). From the world's perspective, this seemed justified, but it was not God's way. God had a better plan to deliver His children from their enslavement. Moses had to be trained and prepared, thus he spent forty years in the desert classroom learning obedience. God's purpose for Moses' time in the desert followed by the Israelite people's wandering is revealed later in Deuteronomy 8:2-4, "He [God] did it to teach you that people do not live by bread alone; rather, we live by every word that comes from the mouth of the Lord."

Jesus spent forty days being tempted in the desert before launching his earthly ministry. He faced his adversary and was victorious over Satan's trials and temptations with God-honoring responses.

It is possible that our trials and hardships are pop tests in God's school of learning to prepare us for an assignment from Him. We may not actually be in a desert, but we may experience similar emotions and be tempted by the same appeals from Satan. The adversary views irrational feelings as opportunities to twist our perspective and delights in misrepresenting God. These may be the very times to draw close to God via prayer and His Word.

Lessons From Job

One of the more well known Biblical examples of testing in God's classroom is the Old Testament book of Job. Here, we learn much about God and Job, from whom all was taken away. We can trace Job's behavior and the development of his perspective during each phase of extreme hardship.

Job experienced extreme hardships in four areas valued most by the world:

1. Health

2. Family

3. Possessions and livelihood

4. Friends

Times have not changed. These are as important today as then. We learn from Job's responses as God allowed Satan to attack Job in each of these areas. The classroom test was whether Job loved God for who He (God) was, or, instead, only for what He did for Job. For thirty-seven chapters Job questions God. He was rebuked and wrongfully accused by his friends. At one point Job was even encouraged by his wife to "curse God and die" (Job 2:9).

Satan challenged and slandered God's integrity by questioning Job's goodness and worship of God. Satan's accusation was that the only reason Job served God was because God provided Job a lifestyle of benefits. Thus, God allowed Satan to start chipping away at each of these areas to refute these allegations and show the faithfulness and legitimacy of Job's worship.

Job's response teaches us that love for God is based upon who He is and not dependent upon blessings of health or material gain. This truth flies in the face of what the world seeks. Devotion to God can be genuine even in the worst of conditions.

Later in the book of Job, God intervened and clearly

and forcefully pointed out His sovereignty. He spoke of the foolishness of Job's questions and the folly of being reminded of Job's self-righteousness. It's noteworthy that God never answered any of the many questions Job asked during the trials. Rather, God correctly reminded Job of who He (God) is and what He has done. Once Job realized that God is God, he rightfully and humbly responded.

> *I have said too much already; I have nothing more to say.* —JOB 40:5

We learn from this exchange that the wrong response to suffering is to question God and to point out the unfairness of our situation based upon our goodness. Also, it is wrong to base all suffering as God's judgment and punishment for sin. The book of Job ends with a humble Job continuing to profess his trust in God that is always the right response to suffering.

Is it possible that God would allow us to be tested by removing those things we value above our relationship with Him? Suffering can be a test of trusting God for who He is and not for what He does. God may allow all worldly sources of hope or strength to be taken away in order to learn to trust completely in Him and Him alone. God responds to such dependence.

Not ignoring the pain, many of the Bible's most significant individuals first had to be broken and taken to the point of complete dependency upon God; once done, God then used that person as His instrument to accomplish His plan and greatest works.

There is much we do not understand but this we do know: God loves us far beyond what we can ever imagine or know during this lifetime even during extreme times of suffering. God's classroom may include our loved ones. Hardship and adversity often comes into the lives of those we love the most. When they hurt, we hurt. In the midst of heartbreaking situations, God often teaches His most valuable lessons.

This truth was described by a Christian parent.

The straightest path to a parents' hearts is through their children. Sometimes that path is filled with pain and anguish when one of your dear loved ones is out of control, suffering, and on a destructive path brought about by drug addiction. We traveled this path with our son.

As parents of three boys, even though they all had the same upbringing, we began to notice the difference in our youngest who struggled with anger, aloofness, and isolation from the rest of the family. We watched as his attire and physical appearance began to resemble the darker side of our culture, and his friends were not of our choosing. All this culminated in our shocking discovery of his addiction to drugs that had led to heroin!

Where had we failed? How stupid had we been not to notice and see the signs? We grew up in the '60s and were well aware of the dropout drug culture! Why did we not see this in one so close to us!

Our son was a drug addict!

We were confused and hurting. We were crushed, not just for ourselves but for our son. What do we do? Who will help us and our son?

As Christians, we turned to God. Our loving God, who had sacrificed His only Son, comforted us and gave us strength and direction through months of tough times. He held us together each difficult and painful step of the way with His amazing supernatural care. There were times when our hearts ached and tears came in buckets as we left our weeping son at rehabilitation facilities. When we didn't know how to pray, our Christian friends held us up and prayed unceasingly.

We were sustained by the promises in God's Word. We held onto promises like those in Romans 8:28-29 that assured us that all things—including drug addiction—works for good for those who love Christ. There were times when all we had was the trust and hope that God was in control and good would come from this terrible experience.

As we came through this, we learned that sometimes you have to experience the pain of watching the ones you love be disciplined and trained for godliness. We also learned that God had much for us, as parents, to learn—most importantly that we have less control than we ever imagined. Our sovereign Father God is in control and knows much better than we how to train and care for our now adult children. And last, we learned that "no discipline seems pleasant and is painful [that's an understatement!], "Later on, however, it produces a harvest of peace and righteousness for those trained by it" (Hebrews 12:11 NIV).

We rejoiced in our harvest of a renewed son, free of addiction and back with the family. He is a joy to be around and together we thank and praise God. God can be relied upon, even in our darkest and most hopeless moments.

However, while we are thankful that our son was renewed and returned to us; we realize that this could have had a very different ending. God is still good and if that had been the result then we are confident that He still would have provided abundant grace to endure and praise Him and give testimony to other parents with wayward children. Yes, God delivered our son, but as noted in Daniel 3:19-20, "Our God is able, but whether He delivers us or not, we still will trust Him."

We have much to learn as God's children. God loves us so much that He allows trying circumstances and pain to enter our life to teach us things we would never learn otherwise.

Admittedly, many hardships and crises test our understanding. We may often find ourselves in the same category as Peter when he questioned Jesus as He (Jesus) prepared to wash Peter's feet. Jesus responded, "You don't understand now what I am doing, but someday you will" (John 13:7). Until then, we have a choice in perspective and our response.

Chapter 10: God's Workshop and Classroom

Summary Points for Reflection

1. God is at work in and around each of His children to transform us into the likeness of Christ.

2. Our lives are God's classroom where He as our teacher shapes and molds us into Christlikeness via various growth experiences often disguised as hardships.

3. Challenging circumstances and pain have the capability to teach us things we would never learn otherwise.

4. These hardships can strengthen and grow our faith.

5. Difficult times challenge us to rely upon God and experience His presence and promises in His Word.

6. Dry times of feeling disconnected or separated from God may be His signal that He wants to spend extended time with you to renew and strengthen the relationship or reveal a task or greater assignment.

7. Our love of God is based upon who He is and not dependent upon blessings of health or material gain.

8. Many in the Bible had to be broken and taken to the point of complete dependency upon God; once done, He then used that person to accomplish His great plan.

9. Adversities and personal losses can test our understanding; however, God is more interested in our trust than our understanding.

Chapter 10: Questions for Meditation & Discussion

1. Describe the following two categories of people:

    Those who know about God:

    Those who know God:

2. God is always at work. In Romans 12:1-2, what does God want to do in His children?

3. What additional insight can be gained from what God wants to do in our lives from the following verses?

    2 Corinthians 5:17

    Galatians 2:20

    Colossians 3:3

    Colossians 3:17

4. How would you respond to one who mistakenly believes that all of life's good deeds and behavior should account for something and earn acceptability and favor from God in this life? Explain your answer.

5. What do the following verses teach about God's standard of our being righteous in His sight?

    Romans 3:10-12

    Romans 3:23, 27-28

    Romans 4:13

6. As you consider all that God has done for you as His child, note the following and select those that are the most meaningful to you. Explain your selections.

- He removed sin. (Psalm 102:12)

- He cleanses and removed any stain of sin. (Isaiah 1:18)

- He completely puts sin and any result of sin behind Him. (Isaiah 38:17)

- He remembers sin no more. (Jeremiah 31:34)

- He stomps our sins underfoot. (Micah 7:19)

- He casts our sins in the depths of the sea. (Micah 7:19)

- He is faithful to forgive us of all our sins. (1 John 1:9)

- He cleanses us from all unrighteousness. (1 John 1:9)
- He gives mercy and grace at the time of need. (Hebrews 4:16)
- His sacrifice was once and for all. (Hebrews 7:27)
- No longer is there any need for offerings. (Hebrews 10:18)
- Jesus perfected us forever. (Hebrews 10:14)
- We are justified to God by Jesus' one act. (Romans 5:18)
- There is no condemnation for those in Christ. (Romans 8:1)
- God's love is permanent and cannot be lost. (Romans 8:38-39)
- You can be assured that your salvation is intact. (John 10:28-29; Romans 5:8-10; 2 Timothy 1:12; Jude 24; Hebrews 7:25; Titus 3:5)

7. What is God doing in your life now to conform you into Christlikeness? Explain.

CHAPTER ELEVEN

HELPING GOD OUT

I'll admit it. I like to get things done. And fast!

I'm a product of my environment. After some forty years in corporate leadership, I'm accustomed to taking charge, making decisions, and implementing a plan. And, in most cases, when I want to take advantage of an opportunity or solve a problem, my motto is, "The quicker the better!"

Waiting was weakness! As the popular ad slogan says, "Just do it!"

While this may sound good in business circles, it is lacking and may be a critical mistake apart from God. Notwithstanding those unique times where action must be taken quickly, the tendency to act quickly without seeking God and His direction often results in getting ahead of Him. There are those who, if the truth were known, spend their lifetimes following this pattern. They may even justify what is done or accomplished based upon the benefits it will bring God or the church.

The pitfalls of this approach were dramatically made clear to me when I retired. I had much to learn about God's agenda versus my own. With retirement, I was free from travel demands and the long days required in my CEO position. I confess that I was looking forward to all the things I could do for God—as if He needed my help!

I began to receive speaking requests and accepted each with little thought or consideration of asking God what He wanted. Each of these was ministry related and I assumed each would certainly please God. How lucky God was to have me now that I was available. I prepared presentations for use in various Asian countries to Christian business leaders. The irony of all this was that my topic was "Following God's Agenda vs. Your Own."

Four days before I was to leave for Asia and launch my speaking tour I made a precautionary visit to my doctor to treat some recurring pains. After preliminary testing, I was shocked to receive a report suspecting cancer. My doctor told me that travel was out of the question. More tests were scheduled and all my trips and appearances were canceled. Everything came to a screeching halt.

Why was this happening? Didn't God know what I was going to do? Wasn't He aware of all the benefits for Him?

Extended time alone in prayer and time in His Word opened my proud and arrogant eyes. It was then that like the Psalmist Asaph said in Psalm 73:17, "I went into your sanctuary O Lord and I finally understood." God didn't need my help. I was operating ahead of God. I was on my agenda and not His. I had much to learn.

I had to confess my self-centeredness and accept whatever lay before me. I admitted that with retirement, I had merely shifted gears but was still planning to follow my own agenda and what I wanted. I realized that God wasn't so much interested in what I did as much as He was interested in me, my motives, and my willingness to yield to Him. It was as though He said to me, "Not so fast! If you do this your way and with your own agenda, it is you who will be glorified. Stop and listen to Me! You need to learn some things about Me and My ways. You must do things My way!"

I had to confess that pride had reared its ugly head. Of

course, I always talked about how God was going to be glorified, but implicitly it was all about me and what I was going to do for God. What arrogance and presumption! Repentance was in order and much private time followed with my giving Him His rightful place in my life and seeking His will and direction. God has no appetite for secondhand glory!

Coincidentally, once all my plans were canceled and I began to view things from God's perspective, my doctor called and asked me to come in for a personal visit. That's never a good sign. Arriving at his office, I was ushered into one of those cold, stark little rooms and told to wait as the doctor wanted to talk to me. I knew what the message was going to be, or at least I thought I did. After what seemed like hours, the doctor hurriedly walked into the small examining room with his nose buried deep in my medical file. I was prepared for the worst.

To my surprise, he said, "I don't understand this! You've proved me all wrong! All those tests we did before are now negative!" I asked, "You mean there's no cancer?" "Nope", he replied. I had to laugh! God was at work! As he left the room, he turned and said, "Well, whatever happened, you're different now." He was right, I was different, but not in the way he meant!

My plans were mine. My attempt to mask them spiritually by telling God how much my success would glorify Him was not a Scriptural pattern. The servant doesn't tell the Master; the Master tells the servant. The Bible is filled with examples of folks who tired of waiting for God and launched their own plans to bring victory and glory to God. Each time, they failed miserably.

God is focused on who we are versus what we do. It's not that He doesn't care about our doing; it's simply that out of our being comes doing. We are more prone toward activity and doing; God is more concerned with our being a person who is pleasing to Him. This requires that we seek Him and His ways that often translates into waiting on Him for His agenda. Our plan typically differs from God's, and many mistakenly redefine God as One who exists to help achieve our personal goals. God's ways are not man's ways! We must not get ahead of God; we must seek and stay on His agenda.

God's unchanging mission is to bring glory and honor to Himself. In accomplishing this mission, it may include our success or failure from the world's perspective. There may be times of waiting or a path of adversity that seems undesirable and contrary to human wisdom. It's all about Him and His mission.

To accomplish His plans and purposes He cares about the what, how, and when of our activities.

We must not get ahead of Him.

Chapter 11: Helping God Out

Summary Points for Reflection

1. Our lives as Christians are not about our personal agendas; instead it is all about God and our mission to bring honor and glory to Him.

2. Notwithstanding those unique times where action must be taken quickly, the tendency to plan and act without seeking God's direction results in getting ahead of Him.

3. Getting ahead of God typically translates into living by our own agenda versus God's.

4. This pattern of acting apart from God masks self-centeredness and pride. God finds no pleasure in second-hand glory.

5. Even if our agenda appears to be good and beneficial, the servant doesn't tell the Master; the Master tells the servant what, how, and when something is to be done.

6. The Bible contains many failed examples of those who tired of waiting for God and launched their own plans to bring victory and glory to God.

Chapter 11: Questions for Meditation & Discussion

1. Why do we typically run ahead of God?

2. What is the teaching in Psalm 46:10 and Isaiah 30:18?

3. What can we learn about waiting from Micah 7:7?

4. What is the principle contained in the following verses?

   Deuteronomy 1:6-7

   Exodus 14:15

   (Note: These actions only took place when there was a clear command or assurance from God as to what was to be done.)

CHAPTER TWELVE

MARKS OF SPIRITUAL MATURITY

In Christian circles, we often hear the descriptive phrase "spiritual maturity." Individuals are often described as being spiritually mature, or, in certain cases, lacking in this desirable trait. Teachers routinely include this as one of their teaching goals. Church leaders may be appointed using this as selection criteria. But what does this mean?

I asked several Christians what spiritual maturity meant to them. Their answers varied. For example:

- "Someone who knows the Bible and lives it."

- "One who's been around a long time in the church and knows a lot about the Bible."

- "A leader who is living like Jesus."

- "A wise person who makes decisions Biblically."

- "An older person who walks the talk."

As is obvious, spiritual maturity means different things to different people. Admittedly, there are many desirable characteristics contained in the responses listed above, but any one answer by itself falls short in giving us a clear picture of how the Bible defines a mature follower of Christ.

It is helpful to keep in mind what is meant by the term mature or maturity. The dictionary defines this as either an attained state of being, or as a process to achieve such a condition. For example, one who is mature or has achieved maturity is one who:

- Has realized a condition of full development, completeness.
- Has completed natural growth and development.
- Has undergone a process that achieves a desired state.
- Has suitable characteristics.

Applying these secular descriptions of maturity, we can state three truths about our maturity in Christ:

- Spiritual maturity is a lifelong, on-going development process toward becoming more like Jesus in every aspect of life.

- The desired state of full maturity and Christlikeness will only be achieved when we are glorified and joined with Jesus.

- Spiritual maturity exhibits Christlike behavior, speech, values, priorities, and Biblically compliant and consistent decisions.

The Apostle Paul alludes to this growth process in his encouragement to the Philippians, "I am certain that God, who began the good work within you, will continue his work until it is finally finished on the day when Christ Jesus returns (Philippians 1:5-6).

During my tenure at Transamerica, our advertising logo and symbol was the tall pyramid-shaped building located in San Francisco. It is the city's landmark and easily recognized in the skyline of the city. For a short time, our ad tagline was "The Power of the Pyramid Working For You." It sounded catchy and typically was posted along with our well-known pyramid-shaped building. At one point we sought feedback of the effectiveness of our ads from a consumer group. We were surprised when we asked if they had heard or seen our ad tagline. The group quickly responded positively, but added the surprising comment, "Yes, we know the power of the pyramid is working but don't have a clue what it's working on." Suffice to say, we changed our tagline.

The power of God is working in us, and unlike our advertising, He is not silent in telling us of His desired result. Once we make the decision to accept Christ as Savior, then God begins His work of transformation. This results in the creation of a "new person" as described in 2 Corinthians 5:17, "This means that anyone who belongs to Christ has become a new person. The old life is gone; a new life has begun!"

Romans 12:1-2 gives more information about this new person, "I plead with you to give your bodies to God because of all He has done for you. Let them be a living and holy sacrifice—the kind He will find acceptable. This is truly the way to worship Him. Don't copy the behavior and customs of this world, but let God transform you into a new person by changing the way you think. Then you will learn to know God's will for you, which is good and pleasing and perfect."

Considering these passages, we can identify additional truths about the process of spiritual maturity.

1. When we became a Christian, we became a "reborn" new person.

2. As we grow, the old behavior patterns and the way we thought are changed and to be put off as part of the spiritual maturity process.

3. We have begun a new life.

4. God urges and pleads with us now to sacrifice our selfish motives.

5. It now is all about God and His glory in every aspect of our life.

6. The right way to worship God is by living selflessly.

7. God will change the way we think and look at life.

8. All of these changes are good, pleasing, and perfect to God.

Likewise, spiritual maturity can be expanded to include the following characteristics:

1. Becoming independently dependent on God's Word and able to feed one's self for spiritual growth.

2. Developing the character of Christ.

3. Having a growing intimate loving relationship with Christ.

4. Developing a Christlike servant attitude and displaying a life expendable for God's use and purposes.

5. Viewing life's circumstances from God's eternal perspective and mission.

6. Living a life that consistently honors and brings glory to God in every situation.

7. Living a life that exhibits the Scriptural traits of an obedient disciple of Christ.

8. Exhibiting the qualities of the fruit of the Holy Spirit: love, joy, peace, patience, kindness, goodness, faithfulness, gentleness, and self-control (Galatians 5:22-23).

Implicit in all of these is the realization that our lives as Christians are not about us and our personal agendas; instead it is all about God and our mission to bring honor and glory to Him. Our endurance and continued witness in the midst of life's storms reveal God's glory and strengthens our own faith for greater tasks.

Our response during times of hardship reveals much about our spiritual maturity. God is glorified by a response that should differ greatly from that of the world. From God's perspective, He expects His children to respond in a manner foreign and seemingly ridiculous to the world's thinking. "We can rejoice, too, when we run into trials and problems, for we know that they help us develop endurance. And, endurance develops strength of character, and character strengthens our confident hope of salvation. And this hope will not lead to disappointment for we know that God loves us" (Romans 5:3-5).

Such rejoicing is only possible if we bring our personal view and perspective in line with God's desire and are able to sense His purpose for our spiritual growth and maturity. Failure to do this will hardly produce rejoicing for trials and, in fact, may generate ungodly reactions. If this happens, then Satan has the victory.

James also underscores the importance of this truth, "when troubles come your way, consider it an opportunity for great joy. For you know that when your faith is tested, your endurance has a chance to grow. So let it grow, for when your endurance is fully developed, you will be perfect and complete, needing nothing" (James 1:2-4). Those are challenging words that give us a different perspective and meaning to times of hardship.

These verses tell us that endurance is the secret of being complete and needing nothing during times of trouble. Our ability to endure rests on a strong and tested foundation of faith. Life's trials can be God's instruments through which He strengthens our faith, and thus our endurance. This is why James tells us to look upon troubles as opportunities for great joy (James 1:2).

This puts suffering and adversity into a very different category contrary to the world's perspective. God's pathway to maturity is not easy and contradicts everything the world values.

Unfortunately, our culture has redefined God's path to include comfort and pain-free lifestyles. You will not find this in God's Word. What He does provide is the strength and resources to endure and rise above life's adversities and crises.

Scripture includes many examples of responses to hardships and adversity, both mature and spiritually immature. We need only look at the Israelites after their miraculous deliverance out of Egypt and journey to God's Promised Land. God powerfully and visibly demonstrated His power to Pharaoh and the Egyptians, which resulted in the Israelites release and departure from Egypt. During this time, Moses delivered God's promises to the people repeatedly assuring them that He [God] had heard their cries. One might think that such declarations followed by God's supernatural acts would have produced a high degree of faith and reliance upon God. Such was not the case.

The Israelites had been released from four hundred years of enslavement and were free at last! One can imagine the celebration among them as they journeyed to a land promised by the only true living God. Their joy evaporated in the scorching heat and desolation of the desert. Conditions were intolerable for people not used to desert living. They were uncomfortable and in a strange, harsh environment. As if this wasn't enough, upon discovering that the Egyptians were pursuing them, they became afraid and angry with Moses and God.

While enslaved, the Israelites wanted deliverance and for years pleaded for God to act; but they wanted God to act in a way acceptable to them and their agenda. When God's plan differed, they cried out, "Why did you bring us out here to die in the wilderness? Weren't there enough graves for us in Egypt? What have you done to us? Why did you make us leave Egypt? It's better to be a slave in Egypt than a corpse in the wilderness!" Their mistaken conclusion led to an ungodly response. They assumed the worst and attacked God, not a godly response in a time of adversity.

In spite of the people's actions, God acted and revealed His unchanging plan that continues even today as described in Exodus 14:17-18, "My great glory will be displayed…When My glory is displayed…[all] will see My glory and know that I am the Lord!" Again, God's mission was to bring glory to Himself.

There are times in our lives when like the Israelites we cry out for God to help us and remove our suffering. However, we have our own idea and plan for how such deliverance should look or take place. The Israelites pleaded for God to act, but they wanted God's actions to fall into line with their own desired way of accomplishing their prayers. When God didn't perform as expected, they reacted in an ungodly manner.

Spiritually mature Christians do not regard God as one to be summoned to help with their agenda. They desire that God play a much greater role.

Chapter 12: Marks of Spiritual Maturity

Summary Points for Reflection

1. Having made the decision to believe in and accept Christ as Savior, God begins His work of transforming us into Christlikeness.

2. Growing in Christlikeness and growing in spiritual maturity is a lifelong process.

3. The desired state of full maturity and Christlikeness will only be achieved when we are glorified and joined with Jesus.

4. Spiritual maturity exhibits Christlike behavior, speech, values, priorities, and Biblically compliant and consistent decisions.

5. Spiritual maturity exhibits the following characteristics:

   - Having regular disciplined times in prayer and God's Word, the Bible.

   - Growing spiritual character qualities of love, joy, peace, patience, kindness, goodness, faithfulness, gentleness, and self-control. (Galatians 5:22-23)

   - Having a growing intimate loving relationship with Christ.

   - Developing a servant attitude that displays a life expendable for God's use.

   - Viewing life's circumstances from God's eternal perspective and mission.

   - Living a life that consistently honors and brings glory to God in every situation.

   - Exhibiting the Biblical traits of an obedient follower of Christ.

- Playing an active role in God's Great Commission.

6. Life's trials can be used by God to strengthen our faith, and move us forward in maturing spiritually.

7. Our response during times of hardship plays an important role in this transforming process.

Chapter 12: Questions for Meditation & Discussion

1. Who or what is your primary source of spiritual development and growth?

2. What does it mean to become independently dependent on God's Word? Explain.

3. James 1:2 talks about "rejoicing" when encountering various trials and problems. What is the basis of rejoicing? List the potential qualities that may result from adversity. Rejoicing during and after a hardship is not a natural occurrence. What is necessary in order to produce rejoicing? How does this happen and how can it be developed?

4. What are the promises or truths in the following verses?

> Psalm 14:2
> Psalm 28:7
> Psalms 37:23-24
> Psalms 56:3-4
> Psalm 119:71
> 2 Corinthians 4:16-17
> 1 Peter 5:10
> Hebrews 13:5

5. Undoubtedly, Christians and non-Christians alike feel

pain and suffering which accompanies many adversities. To deny this is unrealistic. However, their reaction and perspective differs. Describe how.

- Contrast how the world reacts to suffering and hardship versus a spiritually mature Christian.

- Can you recall a Christian who displayed Christlikeness during or after a time of crisis? Describe this situation.

6. What do these verses indicate is God's primary mission and purpose for every believer?

> Exodus 14:17-18
>
> Isaiah 43:7
>
> Matthew 28:19-20
>
> John 15:8
>
> Romans 4:20
>
> 1 Peter 4:11

7. If you accept that God's primary mission for His children centers upon glorifying Himself and playing a role in His Great Commission, then do you also believe that He will do everything possible to mature you to the point of being active in accomplishing this purpose? Explain.

CHAPTER THIRTEEN

BECOMING GOD'S INSTRUMENT

It may come as a surprise, but God is more interested in our Christlikeness than our comfort.

He can use each experience as a growth opportunity to mold us into instruments for his use and purpose. Our response to hardships plays a role in this transforming process. Our usefulness and effectiveness, however, will always be coupled in the context of our character.

One of my Christian friends attends church regularly and routinely talks about his faith. There is just one problem: his personal lifestyle. His character belies his spiritual talk and dulls his effectiveness as God's instrument. There is a word for this: hypocrisy.

Being God's instrument is directly related to our godliness, which includes our character, faith, and consistent walk with Him. Paul instructed Timothy in 2 Timothy 2:20-21, "In a wealthy home some utensils are made of gold and silver, and some are made of wood and clay. The expensive utensils are used for special occasions, and the cheap ones for everyday use. If you keep yourself pure, you will be a special utensil for honorable use. Your life will be clean and you will be ready for the Master to use you for every good work."

Assuming we desire to be considered a utensil for honorable

use, then our growth toward Christlikeness and maturity should be primary. This prompts two important questions:

1. How does God develop instruments for his honorable use?

2. How do we become more Christlike?

There is not one right answer to these questions. They will vary for each individual. God can and does use various means to accomplish His purposes. Undoubtedly, regular time spent in prayer and with God in His Word are uppermost for spiritual growth; however, we must also include the lessons from life's experiences that undoubtedly will include times of adversity and suffering.

When have you matured the most and when has your faith been strengthened the most? Was it when your life was seemingly on "cruise control" with everything going your way or was it during a time when you were facing a crisis and some form of adversity? Inevitably for most, it came during times of suffering that produced feelings of helplessness and hopelessness. These can best be characterized as difficult times when faith and dependency upon God were paramount and tested.

The Apostle Paul speaks of the certainty of God working in each of us, "And I am certain that God, who began the good work within you, will continue His work until it is finally finished on the day when Christ returns" (Philippians 1:6). When we become an instrument fit for His use and purpose, He is able to do "every good work" He has intended.

God didn't give us the Bible to make us smarter or to impress others with our knowledge. The Bible itself speaks of its purpose in 2 Timothy 3:16-17, "All Scripture is inspired by God and is useful to teach us what is true and to make us realize what is wrong in our lives. It corrects us when we are wrong and teaches us to do what is right." Or, simply stated, the Bible is like the GPS in our car; it tells us what road is right; alerts us when we get off track; tells us how to get back on track and teaches us how to stay on the road to our final destination.

God may use hardships to accomplish each of these same four ends to shape our lives and develop us into instruments for His use.

1. Teaches truth—Times of adversity and suffering can draw us closer to God for strength and endurance. This experientially deepens our faith and reveals the truth of His presence and resources accelerating our growth in knowing God.

2. Rebuking and revealing what is wrong—The Greek word for "rebuke" is translated into the English words reprove, correct, convict, and warn. God's rebuking by way of hardships and trials is not an act of punishment. To the contrary, at its core is His love. God's purpose is restoration. His love and desire that we grow prompts Him to allow or use various experiences as gentle rebukes (admittedly, some may not feel so gentle). We must also accept the consequences of reaping what we sow, or the consequences that result from a sinful habit or behavior that needs to be corrected. Once acknowledged and confessed, God graciously forgives our sin (1 John 1:9); however the damage and results may remain.

3. Correction—There may be adversities that God causes or allows in order to change our direction. He also can refine our character by revealing errors and providing correction to get us back on the godliness track. Experiences can prepare us for greater works and to teach us the truthfulness, stability, and power of His Word. Psalms 119:71 reinforces this aspect of adversity; "My suffering was good for me for it taught me to pay

attention to Your decrees."

4. Teaching us to live righteously—Adversity may reposition our lives to live righteously and experience the fruits of God's presence and be used of Him as His instrument. Times of hardship may further equip us for His greater assignments.

This isn't to suggest that every hardship is from God, but no doubt, He can and often does cause or allow events to expand our faith and reliance upon Him. There is a popular TV commercial promoting the use of a cellular telephone service. The message is, "Can you hear me now? Can you hear me now?" I often think that sometimes God may be screaming at us "Can you hear me now?" through various circumstances attempting to teach and train us in godliness.

Jesus used a vine illustration of God, himself, and Christians in John 15. He refers to God as the vinekeeper, Himself as the vine, and Christians as the branches. In this illustration, Jesus said that we are pruned to enable us to be more fruitful. This pruning wasn't prompted because of the branch's failure nor was it an act of punishment by God. It was done in the best interest of the branch to enable it to bear more fruit and to be used for greater advantage as instruments for God.

During times of hardship, we may hear well-meaning Christians encouraging fellow believers by paraphrasing portions of Romans 8:28 saying, "Well, you know God causes everything to work for good." No doubt, God can certainly provide deliverance; however this can also create an expectancy that life will return to normal. The unspoken question that must be considered is, "Who determines what is good?"

While understandable, "good" to us is most often self-centered and singularly focuses on restoring comfort or healing and deliverance from the painful experience. Without question,

God can and often does grant such good, but it would be wrong to assume mistakenly that God's "good" is always characterized by reinstating the status quo. Doing so can create an unrealistic and unbiblical perspective and expectation, not to mention a misguided presumption about God. This can produce Christian casualties.

God's pruning as mentioned earlier in John 15:2 may fall within the scope of "everything working together for good." This can be painful, but the desired outcome must be viewed through the lens of his mission, which is to bring honor and glory to Him or advance His Great Commission. Does it make us more Christlike and more effective for His work and mission, or to possibly prepare us for a new godly assignment?

It's only when we apply godly wisdom to life's circumstances that we can say and believe James 1:2, "When troubles come your way, consider it an opportunity for great joy." This "great joy" can only come in realizing that such troubles are opportunities to bring glory to God by our response. Without such a perspective, this verse makes no sense.

Nowhere in Scripture, including this verse in Romans 8, does it state that all things are good; rather, that all things work together for good. Pain, disease, persecution, accidents, and even death are not good in themselves. The teaching is that God can work all things for His ultimate good. God controls the process. He also can take painful evil acts directed toward his children and turn them into good.

We are not immune from hardships but we can be assured that He is in control and can use our experiences for His good purposes and glory. Who knows what great things God will accomplish through the trusting acts of obedience by His children through times of adversity? As the Psalmist says, "Everything He [God] does reveals His glory and majesty" (Psalm 111:3).

As followers of Christ, there may be times when we experience significant pain and are unable to understand why or to see the good that might contribute to God's mission. It is during these times that we must trust God and His character rather than our own ability to understand. God can accomplish amazing things via hardships; many that may only be realized in retrospect.

This was certainly true for my cousin who was like an older brother to me. He had a severe diabetic health condition that caused intense pain and numerable diabetic comas that would strike without warning. The last few years, as his condition worsened, it became obvious that his time was short.

After his death, when calls were made informing friends and family, one of the comments made by his employer summed up and gives indication of God's purpose for his diseased condition.

At work, we all knew about his illness and loved him and tried to look after him. We also recall the one thing he always did with everyone he met. He would ask them if they knew Jesus. If not, he told them about his relationship with Christ.

What a testimony during a critical adversity!

My cousin hated his condition, but his failing health created a mindset focused on his eternal destiny. This resulted in him telling everyone about Jesus. Who knows how many were influenced by him and perhaps even became believers?

The world would view this situation with sadness and sorrow over his lifetime of suffering. By contrast, God and Jesus greeted him upon his entrance into heaven with the words we all should strive to hear, "Well done, my good and faithful servant!"

Others Are Watching

In addition, we should always be mindful of what God may be doing in the lives of others who are secretly watching our behavior and reaction at times of crisis. They may be watching to see if our Christianity really works. Well-known Christian author and pastor, John Stott, called attention to this need.

Christlikeness is not only what God wants to see in His people, but also what the watching world wants to see. The name of Jesus is on our lips. We speak of Him; sing of Him; pray to Him; bear witness to Him; therefore the world has a right to see in us this Jesus of whom we talk so much. Nothing hinders the testimony of the Christian church more than the wide gap between our claims and our performance—between the Christ we proclaim verbally and the Christ we present visually.[25]

We see this in Daniel's experience with the evil King Darius. The king's officials, jealous of Daniel, devised a sinister plot that resulted in Daniel being thrown into a lion's den. The king knew of Daniel's faith. He no doubt watched Daniel closely. Daniel 6:19-20 describes King Darius running to the den the next morning shouting, "Was your God, whom you serve so faithfully, able to rescue you?" Scripture tells us that Daniel emerged without a scratch!

The king's question resounds loudly in our society today, "Does Christianity work?" "Does God make a difference?" The answers to these questions are seen in our behavior and godly reactions to adversity. In this regard, we can be the instrument that testifies of God's greatness and provision to a lost world.

This certainly is true for someone who endured pain and suffering for years. We tend to think of adversity as a singular event. There is another category equally painful and, apart from God, has the potential to negatively impact an entire life. Painful events or abuses that occurred in childhood have the ability to wound and render victims incapable of developing spiritual maturity.

This reality is best explained from one who walked down this path during childhood and emerged victorious only through the power of God's Word and His intervention in her life. Her testimony brings to mind the response of Joseph to his brothers who abused and discarded him, "You intended to harm me, but God intended it all for good. He brought me to this position so I could save the lives of many people" (Genesis 50:19-20).

As she tells her story, it's important to note that God did not cause or create her painful family situation. Jesus was asked in John 9:3 if blindness was the result of sins. Jesus taught to the contrary, the blindness occurred so that one day we all might see the power of God at work in Jesus. Her testimony reveals God demonstrating the power of His Word to heal her youthful wounds and to use her as His instrument for His glory in the lives of others.

Growing up should be fun. For me, it wasn't.

Childhood should be filled with wonderful times; memories of loving parents and relatives; special times of fun-filled gatherings with hugs and kisses, games and picnics; parents and relatives cheering you at sporting events; vacation trips, laughter, joy, encouragement, and safety. The family home should be a special place of security and protection and filled with fun and love.

Mine wasn't!

As a child, I thought it was normal to have an alcoholic and abusive parent along with several aunts and uncles who were also alcoholics. My dad was an alcoholic, so I never knew when he would come home drunk. I lived in constant fear that produced a life of growing insecurity.

When drinking, my father would verbally attack me using words that cut deeply, instilled fear, and belittled, blamed, and humiliated me. I was too young to know that his lashing out was driven by his own weakness, failure, and lack of responsibility. I was a convenient and readily accessible target for his wrath. Each episode hurt.

I was confused and suspected he was wrong, but to keep peace in our home, I would apologize for each imagined offense—and there were many! Rules were fluid and changed each day. A parent should be the loving protector of children, but my father became my accuser and abuser. Home did not feel like a safe place. I was growing up in constant fear.

I was a good student and school soon became my safe place and an escape from the drama and pain at home. However, I could not escape the painful effects that I carried with me each day. I remember my fourth grade in elementary school as being the time when I was at my lowest. I was nine years old, distraught, and felt no one cared and maybe my father was right about me. This was not leading me down a good path!

When I was at my lowest, a person came into my life who began to turn me around. My schoolteacher was a loving, Christian woman and her unconditional love saved my life that year. I threw myself into school activities and responded to her help, encouragement, and support. I knew that when I did well, I would be appreciated.

No doubt, my teacher's love came at a critical time in my young life, however, my starving for love and appreciation that I never received at home produced a different and equally destructive approach to life. I was very subtly adopting a philosophy geared toward becoming a people pleaser. My driving force was to seek praise in order to feel good and validate my value as a person. Inside I continued to have constant feelings of shame and low self-worth. These were permanent scars that I carried into my adulthood.

Later when I became a Christian and began to grow in my personal, intimate relationship with the living God through His Son, Jesus Christ, I thought all the hurts of my childhood would be put behind me and life would be easier and more peaceful. Even though knowing Him personally eased the routine hurts and bumps of daily life, there still was a "hole in my soul" that needed attention. Something was wrong deep inside me.

My marriage was my way to escape from my home and I spent several years using my own methods for finding love while neglecting the home that my husband and I were trying to build. The early years of our marriage can best be described as an "armed truce," i.e., a marriage in name only.

Into my confused life, God brought another couple who knew the importance of God's Word and modeled for my husband and me how to study and apply God's Word to our lives and helped us write it on our hearts via a disciplined system of Scripture memory.

The change was slow. As we grew spiritually and emotionally, our marriage also began to experience healing. Those nagging feelings of insecurity and trying to please others were slowly being replaced by responding to God's love and a growing desire to please Him. However, the effects of my childhood didn't go away without a struggle. My desire to please God along with my lingering need to please others caused me to overcommit. I confused growing spiritually with always saying, "Yes", to any project that appeared to have God's stamp on it—worse, I expected the same from others. This caused difficulty in friendships, a need to control and lead, my own spiritual burnout, and feelings that I could never be good enough. I was trying to earn my heavenly Father's approval as a substitute for the love I never had from my abusive and condemning earthly father.

My hectic schedule was interrupted with needed surgery and I was sidelined for a few weeks. It was as though God realized that I wasn't slowing down, so He intervened and put me in a position where He could communicate. During this time God directed me to address the pain of my past.

Although I was not an alcoholic, I enrolled in a Christian program designed for those recovering from addiction. The program was immersed with God's Word and over time God worked in my life. I was released from the terrible lingering effects of my childhood experiences by the power of His Word and my trusting in Him, His promises, and His love.

My childhood was painful and I still bear those scars, but God has healed those wounds and is now using my experience and the victory He provided for His glory. Ministry doors have opened as I've discovered many with similar backgrounds.

With God's leading, I have developed a ministry of helping others through a Christian treatment center and a Christian counseling service for other women in my church and community.

I thank Him every day that I am no longer the fearful person I was when He found me—He reached from on high, *"He took me; and He drew me out of many waters."* —PSALM 18:16 NASB

Good soldiers are not made in the barracks or on the parade ground but instead on the battlefield enduring pain and tough times and emerging victoriously. Likewise, God's instruments victoriously bear the scars and wounds of adversity from the battlefield of life.

Chapter 13: Becoming God's Instrument

Summary Points for Reflection

1. God didn't give us the Bible to make us smarter or to impress others with our knowledge; rather He gave it to change our lives.

2. God uses various means to accomplish His purposes; included are His use of people as instruments.

3. God is more interested in our growing to become more like Christ and becoming an instrument for His use and glory than our comfort.

4. Being God's instrument is related to our godliness, which includes our character, faith, and consistent walk with Him.

5. Times of adversity can be used by God to grow our faith and prepare us as instruments for God's use.

Chapter 13: Questions for Meditation & Discussion

1. In 2 Timothy 2:20-21, the Apostle Paul compared two different utensils, those made of wood or clay and those special instruments put aside for honorable use. Which best describes your present condition and why?

2. What would be your answer to the question, "How can I grow in spiritual maturity and godliness?"

3. What is the truth as contained in each of the following verses?

> Philippians 1:6
>
> Colossians 1:9-10
>
> Colossians 2:6-7
>
> 2 Timothy 2:1-7
>
> Ephesians 4:1

4. What does Psalms 119:71 say about one of the outcomes of adversity?

5. How does the good as promised in Romans 8:28 differ from man's definition of good? What is the possible danger and error of misinterpreting this verse and expecting all things to work together for man's definition of good?

6. What do the following verses reveal about the ways of God?

> Isaiah 55:8
>
> Genesis 50:20

CHAPTER FOURTEEN

FIRM FOUNDATION FOR A FRANTIC WORLD

L iving in California is a year-round adventure.

We have four seasons: fire, earthquake, mudslide, and smog! Coming from Texas required some serious adjustments. Earthquakes in particular demand constant attention. Most folks are unaware that the Los Angeles area has well over a thousand earthquakes each year; however most are small and go unnoticed. Buildings and homes must include more stringent supports able to withstand the more intense tremblers. It all starts with the foundation.

The importance of the foundation was evident when we recently added onto our home. I couldn't help but notice the time and effort spent on the foundation. More time was devoted to this than all other work.

The general contractor explained that the foundation was the most important part of any building, and extra effort had to be devoted to assure its strength and stability. He commented that everything his workers would do depended upon laying a good foundation. I recall him saying, "You don't want this to come apart and cause the entire house to fall when we have one of our little earthquakes!" He was right!

I recall watching him on his knees as he checked to make sure the steel reinforcement rods were placed properly before laying the concrete. I asked him what he was looking for while crawling around on his knees. He answered, "You don't want any cracks. Sometimes what looks like something little can bring the whole house down under pressure." Even after his close review, inspectors arrived to sign off approval before work continued. The contractor assured me that laying a good foundation made the rest of the work much easier.

What a great illustration of the Christian life and the importance of building a strong spiritual foundation. God's Word is our blueprint for life providing foundational strength and stability in alignment with the Scriptures. His foundation withstands and weathers life's hardships and serves as a basis upon which to build one's life.

Spending time with God in His Word and in prayer should not be limited to special times of need, but should be a regular part of each day. This daily discipline is the raw material that over time builds lasting foundations that can withstand and endure the "tremblers" of life.

Strong foundations are unnecessary for houses (or lives) that do not experience tests or calamities. Life, however, is filled with various forms of trials and it is critical to have a foundation that withstands such tests. Jesus taught this importance in Matthew 7:24-27, "Anyone who listens to my teaching and follows it is wise." He then described one who fails to listen or follow His teaching as a fool whose house (life) will "collapse with a mighty crash" when adversity comes! Jesus was never one to mince words.

How does one learn and apply the teachings of Jesus? The answer, while obvious, escapes many who limit their exposure to God's Word to Sunday morning sermons. This approach falls short of building a foundation as described by Jesus.

The Navigators, a Christian non-denominational organization, has devoted years of developing mature followers of Christ. One of the disciplines taught is the importance of learning and applying God's Word. To illustrate this truth and its importance, an illustration of a hand is used to identify the various methods of Scripture intake into our lives.

The Hand Illustration: Methods of Scripture Intake[26]
Strengthening Your Grip!
(Used by permission of The Navigators)

Visualize attempting to grip your Bible with your fingers one-at-a-time; starting sequentially with the smallest first, then adding fingers until each is wrapped around and firmly gripping the Bible.

HEARING: The little finger—the pinkie:

This finger represents hearing God's Word. If hearing is the only exposure one has to the Bible, then that person's grasp and grip of the Bible is at risk. It is similar to trying to grip your Bible with only your little finger that is shaky at best and certainly unstable or long lasting. This is akin to limiting exposure to God's Word only at church, listening to Christian radio or recordings. Many walk through life attempting to carry the Word with only their little finger. It doesn't work well in this illustration or in one's life. Strong spiritual foundations are not established using building tools with one's little finger.

READING: The ring finger:

This represents reading God's Word, and is better than only hearing and creates a better grip on the Bible along with the little finger, albeit somewhat unstable and certainly not strong or sustainable. Those who limit their contact with the Bible to hearing and reading seldom focus consistently on application and are prone to miss the nuggets and personal lessons. Most often, the goal is simply to read through the Bible like a book. Again, the grip is unstable and not sustainable.

STUDYING: The middle finger:

This represents studying God's Word. Now a stronger grip is achieved along with the other two fingers because you are now hearing, reading, and studying. However, it still can be subject to loss. At this stage, consistency in application of God's Word begins to take a more serious role. Care must be taken to not treat the Bible as an academic project. God gave us His Word to change our lives by application and deepen our relationship by "knowing" Him, not to make us smarter about Bible knowledge.

MEMORIZING: The index finger:

This represents memorizing God's Word. A stronger grip is now achieved along with the other fingers. Internalization and application are important as verses can be dwelled upon throughout the day and applied for situations as they occur. Temptation can be overcome with verses from memory, and our opportunity to witness is enhanced as we can share verses with others in need.

MEDITATING: The thumb:

This represents meditating on God's Word and is the strongest and most secure grip possible with all the fingers and the hand entirely wrapped around the Bible. It is secure and cannot be lost. Meditation centers upon focusing on a verse and discovering what it says, means, and how it personally applies. This results in obedience and deep understanding with a focus upon discovering the riches of Scripture as God reveals Himself.

Experience proves this illustration to be true. There is a marked difference in perspective and endurance in Christians who have the Word of God embedded into their hearts as a strong foundation. They respond far better to hardships versus those who ignore such spiritual disciplines and basically have weak foundations that cannot withstand life's "earthquakes." As Jesus said, their house comes down with a crash.

Again using the California illustration, preparation for the likelihood of earthquakes and fires is regularly encouraged in the media and by government offices. Public reminders and instructions are visible and frequent. However, invariably there are many who ignore them and as a result suffer and panic when such calamities occur and they most certainly will. Unfortunately, when this happens, the victims are quick to deny accountability, seek out others for help, and blame the government for not taking care of them! Does this sound familiar from a spiritual sense?

How sad to hear a Christian blame God during times of adversity when that person has done nothing to build a firm foundation via personal time with God. Equally sad are those churches that have ignored God's command to "go and make disciples teaching them to obey," and have congregations full of faulty foundations.

I need look no further than my own life as an example. My foundation was shaky at best. For years, I compartmentalized my faith, limiting it to Sunday mornings. My Christianity was of a "stained glass" variety, conducted and restricted behind church windows with little application to the outside world other than attempting to live what I considered to be a moral lifestyle.

During much of my childhood, my faith was routinely shaken during many hours spent in hospital waiting rooms. I cannot recall a time when either one or both of my parents were not preparing for, having, or recovering from surgery. This caused repeated emotional stress for me as many of these were life threatening.

I can remember many times as a young person and an only child waiting alone in cold and stark surgery waiting rooms, emotionally begging God to let my mom or dad survive their respective surgery. In my immaturity and spiritual ignorance, I treated God as if he were my private "medicine cabinet god," on call for each family emergency. After each incident, I would politely thank Him and put Him back in my medicine cabinet. Needless to say, my foundation was weak.

This all changed later in my adult life when I was introduced to the home Bible study as described earlier. The leader was committed to God's Great Commission of making and teaching disciples. For the first time, someone introduced me to the God and Jesus of the Bible and taught me how to study and apply the Scriptures to my life. It was only then that God began His work of building into my life His foundation that continues to this day.

Firm foundations are not built quickly or without hard work and discipline. It takes time and effort. The results, however, may mean the difference between life standing or falling when hardships come. Many sincere and genuine Christians are wounded and may spend years recovering from the lack of God's firm foundation. This is not what Jesus intends.

Foundation building is a choice and it starts with us.

Chapter 14: Firm Foundation for a Frantic World

Summary Points for Reflection

1. God's Word provides a strong and stable foundation for our lives that can withstand hardships.

2. Spending time with God in His Word and in prayer should not be limited to special times of need, but should be a regular part of each day.

3. Limited exposure of hearing God's Word during Sunday morning sermons may be inspirational but falls short of building a foundation as described by Jesus.

4. Firm foundations are not built quickly or without hard work and discipline.

Chapter 14: Questions for Meditation & Discussion

1. Review the parable Jesus told in Matthew 7:24-27. What are the key lessons and how do they apply to you?

2. In practice, how does one build a firm foundation?

3. What do you consider are the chief hindrances to practicing the spiritual disciplines of regular prayer and time in the Scriptures?

4. What steps can you take to eliminate or counter these negative inhibitors?

CHAPTER FIFTEEN

GOD'S PEACE VS. THE WORLD'S PEACE

A s Christians, we are called to be ambassadors for Christ. The Apostle Paul uses this descriptive term for Christians telling us that we are Christ's ambassadors through which God makes His appeal to the world (2 Corinthians 5:20). It's hard, however, to be an effective ambassador and represent Christ if we are in the midst of anxiety with constant worry that approaches desperation due to hardship.

In such cases, God's mission of being glorified is significantly impaired if not nullified. Any difference between Christians and the unbelieving world is lost. The enemy loves to see God's children paralyzed by fear, worry, and the absence of peace.

When times are good, the difference between Christians and moral non-Christians may be hard to detect; however, during times of duress and crisis, the difference ought to be magnified. The difference is God. Gospel opportunities come when others ask why we are so different from the world. As 1 Peter 3:15-16 instructs, "if someone asks about your Christian hope, always be ready to explain it. But do this in a gentle and respectful way." This Scripture assumes that there will be a difference! Unfortunately, for many, there are two problems: Many are not ready, and, worse, no one is asking.

If ever there was a time when our "hope" ought to be recognizable, it is during times of hardship. It may be that we, unfortunately, react much like the world and fail to reflect the peace that God gives during such times. In Philippians 4:6-7 we are instructed, "Don't worry about anything; instead, pray about everything. Tell God what you need and thank Him for all He has done. Then you will experience God's peace, which exceeds anything we can understand. His peace will guard your hearts and minds as you live Christlike."

Five truths stand out in this wonderful promise and often-quoted verse.

1. God's Peace

The first and most obvious truth and promise is the supernatural peace that God gives His children. The world has no such resource. The fact that almighty God, the creator and sustainer of the entire universe, knows everything about us, understands, loves, and will care for us during times of need results in a peace that is beyond all human understanding.

Why would God do this? Consider His mission and the positive impact glorifying Him makes during what the world considers a crisis. The world's reactions differ greatly from the peace that God promises in the worst of situations. As noted earlier, God loves His children far beyond what we might imagine. The Bible tells us that when Jesus ascended He sent the Holy Spirit to come into the lives of all believers. In John 16:7, Jesus calls the Holy Spirit the advocate or comforter. God, as our loving Father, has provided a comforter during times of anxiety.

2. God's Protection

The second truth is often overlooked. God will "guard your hearts and minds." The Greek word translated to the English word "guard" is a military term. It pictures a guard to prevent or withstand an enemy's attack. Who is our enemy? Satan. Scripture defines him as a "roaring lion prowling around eager to eat God's children" (1 Peter 5:8). How can Satan "devour" God's children? His chief weapons are worry, fear, panic, anxiety, and desperation.

The peace the world offers differs from that offered by God. The world's peace is circumstantial and situational. Well-being in the world depends upon self-satisfaction, comfort, and basically having the world meet our every want or need. When adversity strikes, the world's immediate reaction is to seek relief or its removal. Frequently, the world's answer is to provide peace chemically with alcohol or drugs to mask, deaden, or distort reality. This is not a solution and is a dangerous form of denial and escapism.

God's peace is not circumstantial and is promised regardless of the situation or its duration. God can, and often does, provide quick deliverance from adversity; however He may reward our endurance with a much greater benefit. God's way of enduring is not a lonely path and we can be assured that He is with us every step of the way.

This truth is reinforced in 1 Corinthians 10:13 when we are told that God will not allow us to be tempted or tested beyond what we are able to bear but will provide a way of escape that we may be able to endure. The "escape" is not a retreat from reality but rather relief from the emotional pain that so often accompanies hardships. God's promise is that He is a refuge with loving care and strength that cannot be explained or understood by the world.

In the midst of trials, we can be confident that God is with us and is very much aware of what's happening. He delights in comforting us with His presence and promises in His Word. Our ability to endure finds its strength from trusting in Him. This allows us to reflect His peace and visibly testify to His greatness.

3. "...in Christ Jesus"

We shouldn't overlook that God's actions of guarding our hearts and minds from anxiety and other destructive emotions rests in Christ Jesus, not the world or our own personal strength. God is able to comfort and provide a peace far different than what the world offers. However, we must dwell on our position of being "in Christ." During times of need, reviewing what God's Word tells us of His works, attributes, and presence reassures us. The Psalms are filled with outpourings of hurt, fear, and desperation; without exception, comfort and peace come from realigning focus onto God.

4. Pray About Everything and Give Thanks

The Philippians verse includes the promise of God's peace and also tells us what we are to do and not to do—don't worry, rather pray and give thanks. God never commands an emotion without telling us the actions needed that result in producing the desired feelings.

God places no restrictions or limitations on the subject matter of our prayer requests; rather He instructs us to pray about everything. No issue or concern is too small or big to prevent bringing it to our heavenly Father who loves us. There was a time in my own life when I was convinced that God was only concerned with the "big things" of life and in the world. I inwardly scoffed whenever I heard fellow Christians praying about topics that I considered frivolous and too insignificant to bring before God, the creator and sustainer of the universe.

As I explored the Scriptures, I realized that God cares about every aspect of our lives. God brought to my mind the love I have as a human father for my own children and grandchildren. I want these loved ones to talk to me about anything and everything on their mind. I love to hear them tell me about their cares, likes or dislikes, and how they are feeling. Nothing is too small, and I smile when they express their excitement over finding a rock or discover the moon shining brightly in the evening sky. When they hurt and express fear, I love to take them into my arms and reassure them that I am there with them and will care for them and help. Isn't this a smaller reflection of how God loves us?

In Matthew 7:11, Jesus used this comparison of how human parents respond to their children with how God responds to His children, "So if you sinful people know how to give good gifts to your children, how much more will your heavenly Father give good gifts to those who ask Him?" At times of adversity when anxiety and desperation appear, one of God's greatest gifts is the assurance of his presence and love.

We must not miss the important reminder that we are to give thanks for all that God has done. During times of crisis when all about us appears out of control and we conjure up terrible consequences, God wants us to pour out our hearts and be convinced of His presence and love. He wants us to remember and be strengthened by all that He's done for us.

We can learn from God's dealing with the Israelites throughout the Old Testament. Time and time again the people complained, were fearful, or strayed away from the relationship God desired. God continually rebuked and reminded them of all He has done. What a wonderful antidote for anxiety! The next time worry and feelings of desperation appear, stop and pour out your cares and concerns and thank God for what He's done. The more we focus on Him and not us, the smaller our problems become, and peace and assurance follow.

5. Living For Christ

The fifth truth in the Philippians 4:6-7 verse is the phrase, "as you live your life in Christ Jesus." This communicates the importance of staying close to God and developing an intimate and active relationship with Him. God is not some magical "medicine man" that we run to only in time of need. He is our loving Father with whom we have a continuous daily relationship via time in prayer and in His word. This time together enables us to "live our life in Christ" and thus enjoy His promise of peace regardless of the situation. We are also able to serve as effective ambassadors representing Christ in the midst of the difficult times of life.

Many times when disaster strikes, our human response is to seek immediate relief. While this is a natural and expected response, it tends to produce the following familiar pattern:

- God may allow or cause our "roof" to fall, thus creating painful circumstances.

- Our first, and natural, reaction is "I don't like this and want it to stop!"

- We may frantically enlist everyone to pray; that's good; however...

- Our prayer requests are often focused entirely on the difficulty and deliverance.

While this pattern is understandable, we may not stop, look, and listen for what God might be trying to teach or accomplish through this situation. We frequently are so overwhelmed by the problem that we lose perspective. In the midst of our anxiety we tend to give little to no thought to what God may be doing or what He may want to build into our lives or accomplish for His glory. With this in mind, is it possible that many of the items on our prayer list are actually circumstances He allows or causes in order to move us toward Christlikeness, prepare us for a future assignment, display His greatness, or some other purpose for our lives?

Don't misunderstand. Certainly, we should pray honestly and pour out our heart's desire for deliverance, but equally important is praying for endurance, understanding, and seeking God's lessons or higher purposes.

We learn in 2 Corinthians 12:7 that the Apostle Paul had what he referred to as a "thorn in the flesh". The Bible doesn't tell us what the thorn was, but we can assume it was a painful distracting affliction. Paul poured his heart out to God three times for its removal. However, when this was not done, he shifted his focus to the spiritual lesson. In his human weakness and painful condition, he left no room for pride when he said, "I don't want anyone to give me credit beyond what they can see in my life or hear in my message even though I have received such wonderful revelations from God. So to keep me from being proud, I was given a thorn in my flesh." God was well aware of how people might have wanted to elevate and praise Paul for his ministry. This temptation was removed for Paul by his weakened condition. God did not grant Paul's prayer. Paul was continually reminded of his dependence upon God for strength. Only a weakened Paul could magnify Christ's greatness as he continued his ministry.

We must not overlook Paul's concluding statements after talking about his painful thorn, "So now I am glad to boast about my weaknesses, so that the power of Christ can work through me. That's why I take pleasure in my weaknesses, and in the insults, hardships, persecutions, and troubles that I suffer for Christ. For when I am weak, then I am strong" (2 Corinthians 12:8-10). There can be no doubt that the early church was influenced greatly by Paul's Christlike witness and endurance in the midst of his many trials and suffering.

The Apostle Paul was a real person and we can be sure that he was repeatedly asked why God didn't heal him of his noticeable affliction. It presented an opportunity for him to give witness to God by explaining his source of strength and endurance. What an impact that must have had! How often do you see physically challenged individuals rise above their condition to praise and thank God? What a tremendous impact this makes for glorifying God!

Jerry Bridges, Christian author, said it well, "The Christian life is intended to be one of continuous growth. We all want to grow, but we often resist the process. This is because we tend to focus on the events of adversity themselves, rather than looking with the eye of faith beyond the events to what God is doing in our lives. It was said of Jesus that He for the joy set before Him endured the cross, scorning its shame (Hebrews 12:2). We are to look beyond our adversity to what God is doing in our lives and rejoice in the certainty that He is at work in us to cause us to grow." [27]

Scripture is clear in exhorting us to be thankful. It's easy to be thankful for all of God's blessings and the good life we might be living. Being thankful at times of adversity, even to express thanks for the actual situation itself, is something quite different. This cannot be done without a godly perspective and view of His purposes in adversity.

I flinch each time I hear well-meaning Christians exclaim, "God is good!" when describing a granted prayer request. No doubt, God is good, and we should praise Him at such times. However, God's goodness is not dependent upon giving us everything we ask. God is good regardless; we shouldn't reserve those times of proclaiming His goodness only to the moments when He gives us what we request.

Ephesians 5:20 tells us, "And give thanks for everything to God the Father in the name of our Lord Jesus Christ." First Thessalonians 5:17-18 reinforces this with, "Never stop praying. Be thankful in all circumstances, for this is God's will for you who belong to Christ Jesus." What is included in "everything" and "all"? The answer has no limits and includes every circumstance good and bad! To believe otherwise places limits and restrictions on God's power and ability, or at worse, viewing God as our servant and only deserving thanks when

He performs for us.

Does this suggest that in the midst of pain and suffering it is possible to express thanks? Can we thank God for cancer, death, persecution, or a job loss? "Everything" does mean everything. Our thanks and focus however is not on the actual cause of pain, rather it is directed toward the resulting peace, strength, and endurance God provides and how this might bring glory to Him.

Joni Eareckson Tada, quadriplegic leader of a global Christian mission to the disabled, recently highlighted her thanks and peace upon learning of her own breast cancer. She commented that she and her husband were convinced that God was going to use the disease to do something big through her ministry. Moreover, she explained that she is now able to empathize and journey alongside people who are not only struggling with a disability but also with cancer.[28]

God will use any circumstance to accomplish His mission and good work. As painful as the situation may be, it is possible that He will use it to reveal Himself and strengthen our faith, refine us, and build Christlikeness and godly character into our lives.

Adversity, similar to God's Word, can be purposeful, "… that the man [woman] of God may be adequate, equipped for every good work" (2 Timothy 3:16-17 NASB).

Chapter 15: God's Peace vs. the World's Peace

Summary Points for Reflection

1. It's hard to be an effective ambassador for Christ if we are in the midst of anxiety with constant worry that approaches desperation due to hardship.

2. The enemy loves to see God's children paralyzed by fear, worry, and the absence of peace.

3. God's provision of peace and strength during times of crisis magnifies the difference between Christians and non-Christians.

4. The world has no sustainable answers that provide peace, comfort, and hope when experiencing many of life's adversities.

5. During times of crisis when all appears out of control and we conjure up terrible consequences, God wants us to pour out our hearts to Him and be convinced of His presence and love.

6. We need to look beyond ourselves and our adversity to what God may be doing and rejoice in the certainty that He is at work in us and can use hardships for our growth.

7. God can use any circumstances to accomplish His mission and good work. As painful as the situation may be, it is possible that He will use it to reveal Himself and strengthen our faith, refine us, and build godly character into our lives.

8. Adversity, similar to God's Word, can be purposeful, "... that the man [woman] of God may be adequate equipped for every good work."

Chapter 15: Questions for Meditation & Discussion

1. What is the difference between concern and worry? How does Philippians 4:6-7 apply to each?

2. Read Colossians 2:6-7. How can Christians let their roots grow down in Him (God)? What does it mean to let "your life be built on Him"? Describe what this "building process" might look like.

3. During times of adversity, we are encouraged to "stop, look, and listen" for what God may be doing or allowing to shape us into Christlikeness. Indicate how you might accomplish this process during your next hardship.

4. In your own life, what is your typical response when experiencing hardship and adversity? Why? If needed, what would be necessary to change this and what steps can you take now? Explain.

CHAPTER SIXTEEN

REAR-VIEW MIRRORS

W e've all had those times in the car when suddenly we hit something totally unexpected. Our mind immediately thinks, "What was that!?" Most likely, one of our first reactions is quickly to look in the rear-view mirror to see what it was that caused this jolt. We can learn from this illustration when hardships suddenly come jolting into our lives.

Life is not a nice smooth freeway. It's full of speed bumps and potholes. The good news is that God created us with "rear-view mirrors" and He intends for us to use them. He expects us to see where we've been, how He's helped, and to steer and maneuver through life's winding and often bumpy roads. We would do well to use our mirrors to remind ourselves, our families, and others of God's faithfulness.

We must not miss the many times throughout Scripture where God instructed His people to establish a memorial following various events or when He displayed His mighty works and included thoughts as to how they might direct future generations. Remembering what God did was important not only to those witnesses but also to those who would follow. Each miraculous event was important and served to accomplish His plan. Equally important was what each revealed about God and the value and priority He places upon passing this information on to others.

One example of this is found in Exodus 10:1-2 when God gives instructions to Moses. God explained one of the reasons He performed the many miracles culminating in the release of the Israelites by the Egyptian pharaoh, "I've also done it so you can tell your children and grandchildren about how I made a mockery of the Egyptians and about the signs I displayed among them and so you will know that I am the Lord.'"

Also, in Exodus 12:25-27, after God had given specific instructions about establishing the Passover ceremony, God communicated through Moses to the people, "Then your children will ask, 'What does this ceremony mean?' and you will reply." Similar instructions are repeated in Exodus 13:14, "And, in the future, your children will ask you, 'What does all this mean?' Then you will tell them."

Later, God instructed Moses to write down all the instructions that God had given as the people prepared to enter the Promised Land. God explained, "do this so that your children who have not known these instructions will hear them and will learn to fear the Lord your God" (Exodus 31:12-13). Again, when the Israelites crossed the Jordan River into the Promised Land, God instructed Joshua to construct a memorial in the riverbed and said, "in the future your children will ask you, 'What do these stones mean?' Then you can tell them." (Joshua 4:6-7)

God's purposes include remembering what He has done and relating this information to our families so they too "will know that I am the Lord." We do not build stone memorials today; we are living memorials. We are living witnesses to him who lives in us, that He is our Lord and God. God knows our tendency to forget. He repeatedly warned and instructed his people throughout the Bible. He expects the same of us today for three important reasons:

1. To build and strengthen our foundation of faith

God's presence during our lifetime and especially as He

guides us through times of crisis builds a reservoir of faith and encouragement when adversity strikes. Sadly, we are prone to forget or dismiss what God has demonstrated over the years in our own personal lives.

2. To sustain our Christian faith in future generations

God places great value on His children remembering and telling their children and grandchildren of His mighty acts. We have the same responsibility to share what God had done for us. It is far more powerful when our children hear of their family's faith versus just listening to a sermon.

3. To witness to the world of our great God

The world has no sustainable solutions or true answers for life's hardships. When adversity strikes in the life of a non-Christian, a personal testimony as to the difference God made is an effective witness.

Our lives are full of times when God has intervened. It may have been to give His supernatural peace during a time of personal trial. For some, it may have been His miraculous intervention in the shaping of events and outcomes, or His providing seemingly coincidental unexpected provision. It may be remembering a time when despite the pain and suffering, we were able to realize God's greater purpose and bring glory to Him.

An extremely talented Christian friend spoke of his agony of going without a job for over a year. In spite of his networking, countless interviews, and circulating his resume nationwide, nothing happened. He shared his frustration and crying out to God for help. During this painful time, we maintained close contact and focused on God's promises and various Scriptures for encouragement to bolster his faith.

He learned much from his experience and in the process drew closer to God. He trusted Him and His work even when seemingly nothing was happening. Finally, he landed an outstanding position and his trial ended.

In reflecting on his past year, he related to me, "This past year was the toughest and most painful year of my life; it was also one of the best and most fruitful times of my spiritual life. I saw God work and my faith grew like it never has before. I started the year convinced that I would quickly get another job. It was all about me and my talents and resources. God had to break me and take me to the bottom. All my resources dried up. All I had left was to depend upon Him. God did a great work in me. It sounds unusual, but I can now sincerely thank God for putting me through this growth time of my life."

Some years ago I received the surprising news that the Texas company where I worked was acquired and my position was eliminated. In short, I was without a job. To say this was a disruption would be an understatement. My search for a similar position in the surrounding area was futile. It soon became apparent that relocation was necessary.

I reluctantly accepted a position with a larger corporation in, of all places, Los Angeles, California. At that time, none of this made sense. Moving to L.A. was the last place my wife and I wanted to be! Our Texas ministry was fruitful and it seemed contrary for God to allow this to happen. We were heavily involved in our church and community leading Bible studies. This change brought our ministry to a halt. We questioned God and couldn't understand why this was happening. We were unaware that He had a far greater assignment and ministry awaiting us in California.

We moved to L.A. and saw God work in ways that were beyond our wildest dreams. In time we recognized that He had placed us in a mission field with a number of new opportunities. Surprisingly, God orchestrated my career and I soon became the chairman, CEO, and President of one of the largest corporations in the nation. He placed us where He wanted and then provided a platform for even greater witness and influence for His glory than we ever had in Texas.

In retrospect, Texas was our spiritual training ground preparing us for a greater assignment. We were unaware of what God was doing and experienced difficult times with the loss of job and the pain of a relocation away from friends, family, and ministry. This was one of those times when God asked us not to understand, but to trust Him as our loving Father.

We learned from this experience and trusting God and His work even when we were unaware of His plans. As we reflect on this experience it reinforces our faith and confidence.

God's instructions and emphasis upon our remembering to bolster our faith and then to pass our experiences onto others has not changed. He continues to place importance and value on our not forgetting Him and sharing who He is and what He's done in our respective lives.

We are living memorials for all that God has done. When hardships appear, He is pleased when we remember Him and His enabling strength to endure; He is pleased when we recall how He was at work even when we were unaware of His presence; He is pleased when we pass these times along and share our memorials with our children, grandchildren, and others.

Each of us needs to prepare a list of those unique times when God's presence and His working was evident in our lives. Writing down key events or decisions with dates in the back of your Bible is one helpful way to memorialize them. Beside each, note the lessons learned and key Biblical verses God may have used as encouragement during these times. Reviewing this over time will prove most valuable personally and will also provide a resource to share with others during their times of need.

We must be faithful never to forget to use our "rear-view mirror."

Chapter 16: Rear-view Mirrors

Summary Points for Reflection

1. God created us with "rear-view mirrors" and He intends for us to use them. He expects us to see where we've been, how He's helped, and to steer and maneuver through life's winding and often bumpy roads.

2. The Bible is filled with times when God instructs His people to erect memorials so they would not forget His work. We do not build stone memorials today; we are living memorials. We are living witnesses to Him who lives in us, that He is our Lord and God.

3. During challenging times, our faith is bolstered when we remember all that God has done in the past. God's presence during our lifetime and especially as He guides us through times of crisis builds a reservoir of faith and encouragement when adversity strikes.

4. God is pleased when we pass these times along and share our "memorials" with our children, grandchildren, and others.

5. It is far more powerful and encouraging when others hear of what God has done for us versus just listening to a sermon.

Chapter 16: Questions for Meditation & Discussion

1. Looking back over your life, what significant "memorials" have you experienced that are worthy of remembering and represented major crossroads or times when God did a significant work? List and explain the lesson(s) learned for each.

2. What is the value of recording your "living memorials"? What can you begin to do to memorialize these for yourself and sharing with others?

CHAPTER SEVENTEEN

THE DISEASE OF ME

One of the chief characteristics of maturity is the realization that life doesn't revolve around self.

Speaking to classes at a nearby university is one of the more enjoyable activities that I do on a regular basis. It's a pleasure to speak to students preparing to enter the marketplace and to share with them my lessons learned from over forty years in the corporate arena. One of the key points that I stress is that whether in a business environment or in their personal lives, it's not about them!

Our culture has been stricken with the "disease of me." It's contagious. Its symptoms are viewing the world through the lens of self; its most observable side effect is the tendency to see people and things in terms of how they either help or hinder what I want, or worse, what I deserve.

Unfortunately, this tendency has spread to many and consequently has impacted both their relationship with God and their responses to life's hardships. God and His purpose are rarely if ever considered. As discussed elsewhere, God created us to have a special relationship with Him; one that brings Him honor and glory. As Christians, our lives are about Him and not us. Sadly, we have lost our God-view of the world. One of the most revolutionary truths is that God is ever-present, engaged, and at work in and around us. This has profound implications.

Unfortunately, many fail to seek Him or, at worse, shut Him out to follow their own wisdom and personal agendas. God is therefore treated as if He's some distant on-call being to be summoned when needed or after all other means are exhausted. What heresy.

God's plan of redemption is to bring us back into a loving relationship with Himself. His plan has a mission that gives purpose and meaning. Our view toward life's difficulties needs to come in line with His. He focuses on relationships and seeks to show Himself to a needy world as the only living and true God. He desires to develop within each of His children a growing, intimate, loving relationship that translates into progressively growing in knowing Him and then reflecting Christ in our own life.

This process only comes when our values and priorities are to seek Him and His ways. This calls for obedience and discipline. For most of us, we don't have an obedience problem; we have a love problem. A lack of obedience is symptomatic of an absence of love. If we truly love someone or something, then we spend time and resources to enhance the relationship. This applies to our relationship with God. To know God is to love God; to love God is to obey God; and to obey God is to bring honor to God.

This sequence is important. As we grow in our knowledge of who God is and what He's done for us, and add that to His many blessings and promises, then a loving relationship develops. We don't dread spending time alone with God via his Word. As we grow in our knowing, our loving also grows.

During my business career, I was privileged to meet several celebrities and sports figures. In my office, I have several works of art and photos of many of these well-known personalities. A few photos include me with these recognizable individuals. I'm often asked if I know these folks. In all honesty, I don't really know them. I only have had brief encounters with them. The truth is that we had a very casual relationship.

Unfortunately, for many, this is reflected in their relationship with God that can be described as surface level and infrequent based only upon convenience. This is surely not what He desires. Is it possible that God may allow or even cause events to bring His children closer to himself?

A Christian friend who leads an extremely busy life is going through a difficult time with his aging mother. Now in a hospice facility, she is devoid of all cognitive signs and living day-to-day in a vegetative existence. No doubt, my friend is experiencing pain not only in seeing his mother in this condition but also because of the demands placed upon him as he works to ensure her good care. At one point, he began to question God wondering why He hadn't taken his mother home. I suggested that he might be asking the wrong question. It may be that this situation is not about his mother; it may be about him and his own relationship with God. It appears that God called his mother to be used as His instrument to lead my friend to assess his own life and become closer to God.

My friend had allowed his busy life to crowd out, if not replace, his personal time of growing in closeness to God via time in the Bible and prayer. The irony of this situation is that many of his activities were church and ministry related. He was obediently "busy for God." No doubt, one side of obedience is activity related, but if our lives are characterized only by activity apart from also growing in personal time with God, something is wrong.

This kind of singularly focused obedience typically produces bitterness, brevity, and burnout. Over time, resentment and bitterness change once-cherished activity into drudgery. This is followed by brevity as the activity is not sustainable and quitting becomes an attractive option. Burnout is followed by the convenient option to escape. Sadly, we see this all too frequently in dedicated church workers.

God is interested in who we are as much as what we do. Who we are involves our motives, values, and heart condition toward God. These will determine what we do and how we react. Lack of time devoted to growing in our love and closeness to God leads to living on our own agendas with self at the center. With this as our primary focus, even outwardly appearing spiritual activities can become contaminated with the "disease of me" and be more self-serving than God-serving. We need to focus on growing our relationship with God and then allow Him to direct our activities in a manner that brings Him honor and glory.

Although admittedly painful, hardships and challenging times are God's primary means of bringing us closer to Him. It's hard to find anyone in Christian history who became great without earning an advanced degree in adversity. Times of tribulation can create a better opportunity than anything else in life to evaluate and strengthen our faith and dependence upon God.

It is easy to conclude that He is good during times of well-being; it is much more difficult to call Him good when all is not going well. To call Him good in the midst of suffering requires knowing Him and His character. This only comes from time spent alone with Him in His Word, allowing Him to provide strength and encouragement via His promises.

> *Our present troubles are small and won't last very long. Yet they produce for us a glory that vastly outweighs them and will last forever. So we don't look at the troubles we can see now, rather we fix our gaze on things that cannot be seen. For the things we see now will soon be gone, but the things we cannot see will last forever.*
>
> —2 CORINTHIANS 4:17-18

The difference between a knife in the hands of a robber and a surgeon is its intent. Both inflict pain; however, one seeks to rob and hurt while the other to heal, make stronger, and useful. Each time life brings us troubles, we have a choice between characterizing God as a robber or a surgeon.

A PRAYERFUL LESSON

I asked for strength that I might achieve.

God made me weak that I might obey.

I asked for riches that I might do more things.

God gave me poverty that I might do better things.

I asked for well-being that I might be happy.

God gave me adversity that I might grow and experience His joy.

I asked for power that I might control.

God gave me weakness that I might be dependent upon Him.

I asked for things that I might enjoy life.

God gave me life that I might enjoy things.

I received nothing that I asked for.

God gave me everything that I hoped for.

My prayers were answered.

AUTHOR UNKNOWN

Chapter 17: The Disease of Me

Summary Points for Reflection

1. One of the chief characteristics of maturity is the realization that life doesn't revolve around self.

2. Lack of time devoted to growing in our love and closeness to God leads to living on our own agendas with self at the center.

3. Even outwardly appearing spiritual activities can become contaminated with the "disease of me" and be self-serving versus based upon our love for God.

4. God is interested in who we are and what we are becoming as much as what we do.

5. Although admittedly painful, hardships and challenging times are God's primary means of bringing us closer to Him.

6. To call God good in the midst of suffering requires knowing Him and His character. This only comes from time spent alone with Him in His Word, allowing Him to provide strength and encouragement via His promises.

Chapter 17: Questions for Discussion & Meditation

1. In your own words, what is your life's purpose as a Christian?

2. God is interested in who and what we are versus what we do. In your own life, how best can you move toward becoming all that God desires?

3. If you lived each day to bring honor to God, what would be different and how would it look?

4. What are three actions or changes you can make that will contribute to your growing in your Christlikeness and honoring God?

The 20 Right Questions

When trouble comes, it would be wrong for us passively to call every hardship "God's will," play the martyr's role, or refuse to examine deeper so that we might consider what God may want to change or build into our lives.

We should not become paralyzed by tragedy or suffer from the paralysis of analysis, but prayerfully ask ourselves questions to discover what God may be doing in or around us.

Always remember, God is active and knows well the details of every experience we encounter.

Twenty questions to ask ourselves in times of adversity:

> NOTE: While all of these are appropriate, we must realize for some it is possible that answers and lessons may only be identified in retrospect or even when we join God in our final heavenly home.

1. Is my hardship a result of the sinfulness of the world?

> *God created people to be virtuous but they have each turned to follow their own downward path.*
> —ECCLESIASTES 7:29

2. Is my situation caused by some weakness in my own flesh?

> *Don't be misled—you cannot mock the justice of God. You will always harvest what you plant. Those who live only to satisfy their own sinful nature will harvest death and decay.*
> —GALATIANS 6:7-8

3. Is this hardship an attack of the enemy?

Stay alert! Watch out for your great enemy, the devil. He prowls around like a roaring lion, looking for someone to devour. —1 PETER 5:8

James 1:12-15 tells us that God never tempts anyone to drive them to sin; He may allow or cause hardships as we've described above for his various godly purposes but sinning is not one of them. Some hardships may be caused by the enemy and typically are designed as James describes to entice us and drag us away from God. The key is not to dwell or be perplexed about "who" caused the hardship but rather to respond in a godly fashion and avoid giving Satan any victory by sinning. The good news is that God uses any hardships for good whether such adversity is of our own sinful design or caused by Satan.

4. Will this situation prevent me from sinning or cause me to repent from a sin in my life?

So then, since Christ suffered physical pain, you must arm yourselves with the same attitude he had and be ready to suffer too. For if you have suffered physically for Christ, you have finished with sin. You won't spend the rest of your lives chasing your own desires but you will be anxious to do the will of God. —1 PETER 4:1-2

5. Is my circumstance a lesson in order for me to learn obedience?

Even though Jesus was God's son, he learned obedience from the things he suffered.
—HEBREWS 5:8

6. Will this situation teach me to start living in a godly manner?

*My suffering was good for me, for it taught me
to pay attention and to live by your decrees!*
—PSALMS 119:71

7. Can my faith be strengthened as a result of this hardship?

*So be truly glad. There is wonderful joy ahead
even though you have to endure many trials for
a little while. These trials will show that your
faith is genuine. It is being tested as fire tests
and purifies gold—though your faith is more
precious than mere gold. So when your faith
remains strong through many trials, it will bring
you much praise and glory and honor on the day
when Jesus Christ is revealed to the world.*
—1 PETER 1:6-7

8. Has this occurred that I might witness and bear more fruit?

*He prunes the branches that do bear fruit so they
will produce even more.*   —JOHN 15:2

9. Am I experiencing this in order that I might comfort others in similar situations either now or later?

*He comforts us in all our troubles so that we can
comfort others when they are troubled. We will
be able to give the same comfort God has given
us.*   —2 CORINTHIANS 1:4

10. Is this situation God's way of moving me geographically or to change jobs or careers?

*A great wave of persecution began that day
sweeping over the church at Jerusalem; and
all the believers except for the apostles were
scattered through the regions of Judea and
Samaria.*   —ACTS 8:1

11. **Is this hardship one of many similar events over the recent past?**

Examine your life for a trend of hardships and similar difficulties that continually reappear. This could be some indication of God attempting to communicate to you about a needed change or improvement in such areas as a need for relocating, changing careers, multiple job losses due to personal or performance issues, refusal to accept accountability for similar recurring problems, relationship problems, etc. Also, are the hardships increasing in intensity or severity? God may be "screaming" for a needed change.

12. **Does my hardship serve to keep me from becoming proud?**

Even though I have received such wonderful revelations from God. So to keep me from becoming proud, I was given a thorn in my flesh, a messenger from Satan to torment me and keep me from becoming proud! —2 CORINTHIANS 12:7

13. **Is my situation a result of me reaping what I've been sowing?**

You will always harvest what you plant. Those who live only to satisfy their own sinful nature will harvest death and decay. —GALATIANS 6:7

14. **Does this situation call for me to forgive or seek forgiveness from others?**

If you forgive those who sin against you, your heavenly Father will forgive you. —MATTHEW 6:14

15. **Is my hardship a result of my witness and identification with Christ?**

Do you remember what I told you? A slave is not greater than the master. Since they persecuted me, naturally they will persecute you.

—JOHN 15:20

16. Is God speaking to me about my priorities?

My actions reveal my true priorities; not what I claim them to be.

> *Seek the kingdom of God above all else, and live righteously, and He will give you everything you need.* —MATTHEW 6:33

17. Is God calling attention to some "idol" in my life that I've placed before him?

> *You must not have any other god but me. You must not make for yourself an idol of any kind.*
> —EXODUS 20:3-4

18. What can I learn in the midst of this situation that might better prepare me for a new and greater assignment from God?

> *Well done my good and faithful servant. You have been faithful in handling this small amount, so now I will give you more responsibilities.*
> —MATTHEW 25:21

19. Does this hardship make me dependent upon others to teach me the importance of responding and helping others in need?

> *Share each other's burdens, and in this way obey the law of Christ.* —GALATIANS 6:2

20. How is my situation an opportunity to give honor and glory to God?

The disciples mistakenly asked Jesus when they encountered one who had experienced a hardship, "Who sinned, this man or his parents that he was born blind?" Jesus answered, "This happened so that the work of God might be displayed in his life" (John 9:2-3). Maybe your time of darkness is happening so that Jesus can be displayed.

Summary Points for Reflection

1. When trouble comes it is helpful to examine the situation deeper so that we might consider what God may be doing or want to change and build into our lives.

2. We should not become paralyzed or over-analyze each situation, but prayerfully ask ourselves key questions to help discover what God may be doing in or around us.

3. It is important to realize that answers and lessons for some situations may only be identified in retrospect or even when we join God in our final heavenly home.

Questions for Discussion and Meditation

1. Describe the most significant hardship you have experienced in your lifetime.

2. Review the many possibilities of how God can or may have used this for His purpose in your life. Explain.

15 Ways to Believe During Times Of Adversity

Adversity, depending upon the severity, can bring anxiety and pain. During this time we are vulnerable. Feelings can give rise to irrational thoughts and mistaken beliefs. These should not take precedent over the truths of the Bible. God's Word and His promises are not conditioned on our feelings. In the midst of trials, consider the range of Biblical truths.

1. **It could be worse; your salvation remains intact!**

   No matter how long or severe our suffering, we can take comfort that every affliction is temporary. Our problems will not follow us to heaven. At most, they may continue through the rest of our lifetime, but even our lifespan is but an invisible speck when placed on the timeline of eternity.

   > *I [Jesus] give them eternal life and they will never perish. No one can snatch them away from me, for my Father has given them to me, and He is more powerful than anyone else. No one can snatch them from the Father's hand.*
   >
   > —JOHN 10:28-29

2. **Others have faced far worse and gone through it victoriously. Beware of pride and the feeling of uniqueness.**

   > *The temptations in your life are no different from what others experience. And God is faithful. He will not allow the temptation to be more than you can stand. When you are tempted, He will show you a way out so that you can endure.*
   >
   > —1 CORINTHIANS 10:13

The issues are faith and pride. The question is whether you believe God or resort to following your own feelings based on how you perceive the situation. It is sad when Christians give up on God and do not believe He has the capability to handle the adversity. These Christians proceed to work it out themselves, often with excessive debt, undesirable relationships, or other ungodly actions.

Be aware that God may again allow another hardship in order to teach the same lesson missed from the first.

3. No failure is final!

Our present troubles are small and will not last very long. Yet they produce for us a glory that vastly outweighs them and will last forever. So we don't look at the troubles we can see now, rather, we fix our gaze on things that cannot be seen. For the things we see now will soon be gone, but the things we cannot see will last forever.

—2 CORINTHIANS 4:17-18

Satan is the great accuser and delights in taking circumstances and convincing Christian that our failures will last forever and our sins disqualify us or remove us from being used in God's mission. What a lie! It is important to realize that since the "battle" for your soul has been won by Christ, then the next best thing Satan can do is to remove you from being used by and for God to influence others.

We all experience setbacks but failure is never final and our loving and forgiving God has made provision for times when we fail due to our own sinful action.

If we confess our sins, He is just and faithful to forgive us and cleanse us from all unrighteousness.

—1 JOHN 1:9

If adversity is the result of sinning, identify the sin, repent, confess, accept God's forgiveness, and press on!

4. **You shouldn't be surprised!**

> *Don't be surprised at the fiery trials you are going through, as if something strange were happening to you.* —1 PETER 4:12-13

> *Do you remember what I told you? A slave is not greater than the master; since they persecuted me, naturally they will persecute you.*
> —JOHN 15:20

> *I have told you all this so that you may have peace in Me. Here on earth you will have many trials and sorrows. But take heart, because I have overcome the world.* —JOHN 16:33

> *Yes, and everyone who wants to live a godly life in Christ Jesus will suffer persecution.*
> —2 TIMOTHY 3:12

5. **God is sovereign; He knows what's going on; He has the power to change it and He loves me.**

> *O Sovereign Lord! You made the heavens and earth by your strong hand and powerful arms. Nothing is too hard for you!* —JEREMIAH 32:17

The more we grow in knowing God and his sovereignty, the more we begin to understand His ways, mission, and His attributes. The bigger God is to us; the smaller our problems become.

6. **God loves you and always has your best interest at heart.**

Until you meet Him in heaven, you will never realize how much God loves you. He gave us His Son, Jesus, and once we became Christians and God restored the once broken relationship, He now pursues us with the hope that we might have a living, dynamic, intimate relationship with Him. As such, everything God does is good and best for us—even when we may not be able to understand or see this at the time of suffering.

> *See how very much our Father loves us, for He calls us His children, and that is what we are.*
>
> —1 JOHN 3:1

7. **God can use your reaction and endurance for His good and glory.**

> *And we know that God causes everything to work together for the good of those who love God and are called according to His purpose for them.*
>
> —ROMANS 8:28

> *So be truly glad. There is wonderful joy ahead, even though you have to endure many trials for a little while. These trials will show that your faith is genuine. It is being tested as fire test and purifies gold—though your faith is far more precious than mere gold. So when your faith remains strong through many trials, it will bring you much praise and glory and honor on the day when Jesus Christ is revealed to the whole world.*
>
> —1 PETER 1:6-7

> *We proudly tell God's other churches about your endurance and faithfulness in all the persecutions and hardships you are suffering and God will use this persecution to show His justice and to make you worthy of His kingdom, for which you are suffering.* —2 THESSALONIANS 1:4-6

When troubles come your way, consider it an opportunity for great joy. For you know when your faith is tested, your endurance has a chance to grow. So let it grow, for when your endurance is fully developed, you will be perfect and complete, needing nothing. —JAMES 1:2-4

8. **Focus on what God may be teaching you or how He may want to use this for His greater purposes.**

Though the Lord gave you adversity for food and suffering for drink, He will still be with you to teach you. —ISAIAH 30:20

We can rejoice, too when we run into problems and trials, for we know they help us develop endurance. And endurance develops strength of character, and character strengthens a confident hope of salvation. And this hope will not lead to disappointment. For we know how dearly God loves us because he has given us the Holy Spirit to fill our hearts with His love. —ROMANS 5:3-5

9. **Even in tough times and when trouble comes, there is time and a way to do what's right in His sight.**

Those who obey him will not be punished. Those who are wise will find a time and a way to do what is right, for there is a time and a way for everything, even when a person is in trouble.
—ECCLESIASTES 8:5-6

10. **You do not have to understand it all. You need to remain faithful to and trust in Him.**

The Lord directs our steps, so why try to understand everything along the way? —PROVERBS 20:24

> *My thoughts are nothing like your thoughts says*
> *the Lord. And my ways are far beyond anything*
> *you could imagine. For just as the heavens are*
> *higher than the earth, so my ways are higher*
> *than your ways and my thoughts higher than*
> *your thoughts.* —ISAIAH 55:8-9

11. Contrary to Satan's devices and schemes, there is hope!

> *For I know the plans I have for you, says the Lord.*
> *'They are plans for good and not for disaster, to*
> *give you a future and a hope. In those days*
> *when you pray, I will listen. If you look for me*
> *wholeheartedly, you will find me.'*
>
> —JEREMIAH 29:11-14

God directed these words to the exiles in Babylon, however He continues to provide the same future and hope for all His children during times of experiencing feelings of being held captive by life's circumstances.

12. With few exceptions, God's greatest instruments in the Bible to accomplish His plans were those who experienced severe adversity.

> *Who are these clothed in white? Where did they*
> *come from? And I said to him, Sir, you are the*
> *one who knows. Then He said to me, These are*
> *the ones that died in the great tribulation and*
> *have washed their robes in the blood of the*
> *Lamb and made them white.* —REVELATION 7:14

13. God will take care of you!

> *And after you have suffered for a little, the God of*
> *all grace, who called you to His eternal glory in*
> *Christ, will Himself perfect, confirm, strengthen,*
> *and establish you.* —1 PETER 5:10

14. You can trust in God's promises and the truths in the Bible and respond to this situation in a godly manner. He will give you strength to endure and will help you at your time of need—of this you can be absolutely sure!

> *For I can do everything through Christ, who gives me strength.* —PHILIPPIANS 4:13
>
> *If God is for us, who can ever be against us?*
> —ROMANS 8:31

15. And ... "this too shall pass!" There is a godly light at the end of the hardship tunnel.

> *For His anger lasts only a moment, but His favor a lifetime! Weeping may last through the night, but joy comes with the morning.* —PSALMS 30:5

As discussed earlier, all of us are emotionally vulnerable and challenged during times of adversity. This vulnerability is fueled by pain and can increase in intensity. During such times, the sincerity and stability of what we believe can be tested. It's one thing to say we believe God loves and will take care of us when all is well, but quite another to believe this when all is not well. We may experience a crisis of beliefs: what we feel versus what we know. This is best described as a battle between errant beliefs driven by emotions versus Biblical truths not based upon how we feel. This is not to deny the existence of pain; it is real. However, in the midst of our distress, we should not allow our emotions to give rise to wrong thinking leading to conclusions contrary to Biblical truth. Our enemy, Satan, rejoices when this occurs. Victory comes from believing and resting on the foundation of the truths in God's Word, the Bible, and finding endurance, strength, and hope. In this regard, it is important that we focus on the Biblical truths as outlined above.

APPENDIX C

15 Things To Think and Do During Adversity

1. Get and understand the facts of the situation. There are times when we refuse to accept reality and avoid or ignore the facts. This possibly occurs when we are afraid, in shock, are lazy, or simply choose to assume a passive posture toward what's happening. Focus on objective facts and avoid "what if" or "if only."

2. Face the facts. Once you have all the facts, ask yourself the proper questions about what God may be teaching you. If possible, take action to address the facts with godly actions.

3. If you have sinned, confess it and receive God's forgiveness, and press on free from guilt.

> *But if we confess our sins to Him, He is faithful and just to forgive us our sins and to cleanse us from all wickedness.* —1 JOHN 1:9

4. Think on God's goodness and faithfulness.

> *The faithful love of the Lord never ends! His mercies never cease. Great is His faithfulness; His mercies begin afresh each morning.*
> —LAMENTATIONS 3:22-23

> *He did not punish us for all our sins; He does not deal harshly with us, as we deserve.*
> —PSALMS 103:10

Don't allow the crisis to so dominate and consume your thinking that you spend more time researching and dwelling on the hardship than with the One who can provide strength, endurance, and victory. Base your trust on God. The circumstance causing the trial and pain if allowed will consume you and may shake your faith. Focusing on the event fosters irrational questions; focus on God.

5. Be more interested in what God knows and is doing versus what other people think. Be selective in seeking help and counsel from Godly friends and resources.

> O, the joys of those who do not follow the advice of the wicked, or stand around with sinners or join in with mockers but they delight in the Law of the Lord. —PSALMS 1:1-2

6. Search for the possible good and do not dwell on the why. Examine the possible sources of the hardship, but do not become absorbed in trying to figure out the why. The key is not to over-analyze why as much as to respond in a godly manner. You may not understand the "why," but you can trust the "Who." You can be assured that God is aware, engaged, and near.

7. Be honest before and with God in your prayers; examine the many times in Psalms when David poured out his deepest emotions and be encouraged that he always came back to God's love and faithfulness. God knows your heart. Pray for understanding knowledge along with His all-sufficient grace and strength to endure with patience and joy.

> We ask God to give you complete knowledge of His will and to give you spiritual wisdom and understanding. Then the way you live will always honor and please the Lord and your lives will produce every kind of good fruit. All the while you will grow as you learn to know God

better and better. We also pray that you will be strengthened with all His glorious power so you will have all the endurance and patience you need. May you be filled with joy always thanking the Father. — COLOSSIANS 1:9-12

8. Trust the promises of God. There may be times when the only hope you have is your trust and reliance upon God and the promises He offers in His Word.

   God is not a man, so He does not lie. He is not human, so He does not change His mind. Has He ever spoken and failed to act? Has He ever promised and not carried it through?

   —NUMBERS 23:19

9. Write in a journal (or in the back of your Bible) a brief description of the ordeal you're facing and the date. Each day record the lesson(s) that God is teaching you, the Scripture references He speaks through, and the victory and insight He brings. This will be invaluable to share with others and serve as a reminder of God's faithfulness for future reflection.

10. Be convinced in your mind with the truth that God loves you far more than you'll ever realize; He deeply cares about you; and He is present with you—even at times when you may not feel that love. His love will never, ever change!

11. Pray, pray, and then pray some more—stay closely connected to God. God desires an intimate loving relationship with His children. Do not seek understanding; rather seek and ask God to reveal His perspective on the situation. Try to step back from your hurting and tell God that you want to see this from His perspective.

The Holy Spirit will minister to you through His Word with promises and assurances and may reveal His purpose. Be attuned to God and what He is doing in your life through this situation. Make any needed adjustments that you sense God desires to bring your life in line with Him and His plan.

12. Absorb yourself in God's Word. During times of grief read the Psalms and how David poured out his heart to God and reflected on God's greatness.

13. Resolve to not give Satan the victory! There may be times when all you have to hold onto is God. He's enough!

14. Take action and do what you need to do with God's leading. The exercise of faith and trust in God does not preclude the use of all legitimate and godly means to address or solve the issue. Faith does not minimize the performance of duty. It is important however that your actions are in line with Scripture and that you are personally spending time with God daily in His Word and prayer.

Twice in the Old Testament God had to rebuke the Israelites to "Get moving; it's time to get off this mountain!" and again to step into the Red Sea as they were hesitant to take that first step of faith and obedience to cross over. Also, consider God's promise that Joshua would conquer the land across the Jordan River. However, before Joshua crossed the river and began his campaign, he first sent spies to check out the situation. Be wise and smart in your actions.

15. Strive to develop the perspective that your crisis is a gift and opportunity from God. Difficulty and crisis is the soil in which spiritual maturity and faith are grown.

10 Steps To Avoid During Times Of Adversity

1. Avoid playing the "blame game" and becoming a self-centered martyr. Do not assume the role of the helpless victim for the world to pity. This is a perverted form of pride and Christians (and non-Christians) often wrongfully cast God as the villain. In a godly manner and depending upon the situation, take responsibility and accountability. God may be dealing with something in your life that needs to be exposed and corrected.

"Do not judge others...and why worry about a speck in your friend's eye when you have a log in your own!" (Matthew 7:1,3).

2. Avoid withdrawing into yourself and cutting off fellowship with other Christians. Stay active and don't shut down your regular activities, ministry, or times of fellowship with others. Do not allow your hardship and crisis to drive you into solitude instead of deepening your relationships. People will be aware of your situation and your endurance and godliness will be a testimony of God's greatness. Also, allow fellow Christians to pray for you and serve you during this time. Don't rob them of this blessing.

3. Avoid disregarding God's Word. Immerse yourself in His Word and allow Him to speak to you via the Scriptures.

Your hardship has your attention. Seek Him now for strength to endure; awareness of lessons He may want to teach you; discernment to distinguish right from wrong actions; wisdom to see things from His perspective; and direction to take for the next steps.

4. Avoid forgetting God's faithfulness in your life. Think back over your life and the many times God gave you victory and upheld you during other tough times.

5. Avoid neglecting your prayer time with God. Pray, pray, and then pray some more; don't dwell on your problem; rather, focus on God's faithfulness and thank Him for His blessings in your life. A good beginning is to search Ephesians 1 and identify and thank God for all He has done in and for you.

6. Avoid so-called man-made worldly quick fixes for deliverance. They may be contrary to God's plan or what He is working in your life. Moses enacted his own solution against the abuses the Israelites were taking from the hands of the Egyptians; he stepped in and killed a slave driver. On the surface, one might argue he was well justified but this was not God's greater plan and Moses wound up spending forty years in the desert learning trust and obedience.

Be sure before you act that you do so being led by God and not by the world's answer for deliverance. Proverbs 3:5-6 warns us to not rely on our own fallible wisdom.

Trust in the Lord with all your heart; do not depend upon your own understanding. Seek His will in all you do and He will show you which path to take.

God's means of maturing us spiritually may require waiting which may enable us to discern the difference between our own self-effort and God's authentic intervention and deliverance. It's a paradox: God may create or allow adversity, and then thwart our self-efforts to resolve the situation so He may provide relief or deliverance. This may be a trial to reveal the true source of our dependency (our own self or Him).

7. Avoid allowing worry and anxiety to control you and lead to panic and desperation!

   Satan delights in seeing God's people be consumed with fear and worry about the future and the unknown. He (Satan) works to conjure up worst-case scenarios that seldom occur and is a master of putting irrational thoughts in your mind.

   Fear and anxiety drive behavior and actions that are wrong or simply unwise. Stay close to God and rest in His peace recognizing that worry and anxiety are not of Him. Do what is right and necessary with God's leading. Write out Philippians 4:6-8 on a small card to carry with you; better yet, memorize it. Review it several times during each day and pray it back to God.

   "Don't worry about anything; instead, pray about everything. Tell God what you need, and thank Him for all He has done. Then you will experience God's peace, which exceeds anything we can understand. His peace will guard your hearts and minds as you live in Christ Jesus...one final thing, fix your thoughts on what is true, and honorable, and right, and pure, and lovely, and admirable. Think about things that are excellent and worthy of praise."

8. Avoid taking actions that may please others but not God. Your circumstances and resulting actions should primarily be between you and God. If your behavior is shaped and determined by others, then you're marching to the beat of someone other than God.

> *Obviously, I'm not trying to win the approval of people, but of God. If pleasing people were my goal, I would not be Christ's servant.*
>
> —GALATIANS 1:10

9. Avoid obsessing over the world's injustices. Acknowledge that God will deal with evil in His own way and according to His timetable.

> *Don't worry about the wicked or envy those who do wrong. For like grass, they soon fade away. Like spring flowers, they soon wither. Trust in the LORD and do good.* — PSALMS 37:1-3

10. Never give up hope; determine to walk through this with God and continually determine to be thankful regardless of the situation.

APPENDIX E

A Biblical Perspective

The purpose of this book has been to present a Biblical perspective on hardships. Perspective, in general, is derived from assumptions, observations, and facts. Biblical perspective is based upon truth as revealed in God's Word. Throughout this study, many Bible verses are referenced and together provide a foundation upon which a godly perspective is based. It is helpful to first list all of the principles by themselves, and then again with their respective supporting Scriptures.

Foundational Principles

1. God is sovereign

2. God is in control and has your best interests at heart.

3. God is never surprised.

4. God desires that each of his children grow in Christlikeness and He may use life's hardships and adversity to accelerate that goal.

5. God has a role for each of His children in his mission.

6. God is well aware of what's happening and how you feel.

7. God's ways are far different than man's ways.

8. Everything that God does is just, good and reveals His glory and majesty.

9. Everyone who lives a godly life will suffer.

10. God disciplines and trains those He loves.

11. The adversary delights in using hardships and adversity to derail and detract God's people from being involved

and effective in God's mission.

12. Life's challenges reveal our weaknesses.

13. God is ever-present with abundant resources and gives victory over life's trials.

14. Victory may or may not equate to the removal of the hardship.

15. God is purposeful during times of adversity.

16. You must be content to trust God's character rather than your ability to understand. Suffering is a test of trusting God for who He is, and not for what He does or allows.

17. God's peace is not the absence of tribulation, hardship, or suffering; rather, it is His presence in the midst of tribulation.

18. God is ever-present and loves us more than we will ever realize.

Foundational Biblical Principles

God is sovereign.

> *God is not a man ...has He ever spoken and failed to act? Has He ever promised and not carried it through.* —NUMBERS 23:19

> *For I alone am God! I am God, and there is none like me. Only I can tell you the future before it even happens. Everything I plan will come to pass for I do whatever I wish.*
>
> —ISAIAH 46:9-10

> *The earth is the Lord's and everything in it. The world and all its people belong to Him.*
>
> —PSALM 24:1

Be still and know that I am God. I will be honored by every nation. I will be honored throughout the world. —PSALM 46:10

I have made the Sovereign Lord my shelter. —PSALM 73:28

No pagan god is like you, O Lord. None can do what you do? You alone are God. —PSALM 86:8,10

But you are always the same; you will live forever. —PSALM 102:27

Our God is in the heavens, and He does as He wishes. —PSALM 115:3

O Lord...you know everything about me. I can never escape from your Spirit...I can never get away from your presence. You saw me before I was born. Every day of my life was recorded in your book. —PSALM 139:1, 7, 16

God is in control and has your best interests at heart.

O Lord...you know everything about me. I can never escape from your Spirit. I can never get away from your presence. You saw me before I was born. Every day of my life was recorded in your book. —PSALM 139:1, 7, 16

God now knows me completely. —1 CORINTHIANS 13:12B

Your Father who sees everything will reward you. —MATTHEW 6:18

God is never tempted to do wrong and He never tempts anyone. —JAMES 1:14

I will never fail you; I will never abandon you.

—HEBREWS 13:5

Seek the Kingdom of God above all else, and live righteously, and He will give you everything you need. —MATTHEW 6:33

So if you sinful people know how to give good gifts to your children, how much more will your heavenly Father give good gifts to those who ask Him. —MATTHEW 7:11

God is never surprised!

For I alone am God! I am God, and there is none like me. Only I can tell you the future before it even happens. Everything I plan will come to pass for I do whatever I wish.

—ISAIAH 46:9-10

The Lord's plans stand firm forever; His intentions can never be shaken. —PSALM 33:11

He knows the secrets of every heart.

—PSALM 44:21

For your Father knows exactly what you need even before you ask Him. —MATTHEW 6:8

God desires that each of His children grow in Christlikeness and He may use life's hardships and adversity to accelerate that goal.

Don't copy the behavior and customs of this world, but let God transform you into a new person by changing the way you think.

—ROMANS 12:2

Anyone who belongs to Christ has become a

new person. The old life is gone; a new life has begun. —2 CORINTHIANS 5:17

My old self has been crucified with Christ. It is no longer I who live, but Christ lives in me. So I live in this earthly body by trusting in the Son of God, who loved me and gave Himself for me. —GALATIANS 2:20

Just as you accepted Christ Jesus as your Lord, you must continue to follow Him. —COLOSSIANS 2:6

For you died to this life, and your real life is hidden with Christ in God. —COLOSSIANS 3:3

Whatever you do or say, do it as a representative of the Lord Jesus, giving thanks through Him to God the Father. —COLOSSIANS 3:17

God has a role for each of His children in His mission.

I am certain that God, who began the good work within you, will continue His work until it is finally finished on the day when Christ Jesus returns. —PHILIPPIANS 1:6

The more you grow like this, the more productive and useful you will be in your knowledge of our Lord Jesus Christ. —2 PETER 1:8

God uses it [His Word] to prepare and equip His people to do every good work. —2 TIMOTHY 3:17

God is well aware of what's happening and how you feel.

The Lord still rules from heaven. He watches everyone closely, examining every person on earth. —PSALM 11:4

The Lord looks down from heaven on the entire human race. —PSALM 14:2

I know the Lord is always with me. I will not be shaken, for He is right beside me. —PSALM 16:8

God is greater than our feelings, and He knows everything. —1 JOHN 3:20

God's ways are far different than man's ways.

'My [God] thoughts are nothing like your thoughts' says the Lord. 'And my ways are far beyond anything you could imagine.'
—ISAIAH 55:8

Everything God does is just, good, and reveals His glory and majesty.

How amazing are the deeds of the Lord. Everything He does reveals His glory and majesty. All He does is just and good and all His commandments are trustworthy. —PSALM 111:3,7

You are my Master! Every good thing I have comes from You. —PSALM 16:2

Bring all who claim me as their God, for I have made them for My glory. It was I who created them. —ISAIAH 43:7

Everyone who lives a godly life will suffer.

Here on earth you will have many trials and sorrows. —JOHN 16:33

Everyone who wants to live a godly life in Christ Jesus will suffer persecution. —2 TIMOTHY 3:12

When troubles come your way, consider it an opportunity for great joy. —JAMES 1:2

God disciplines and trains those He loves.

> *For the Lord disciplines those He loves.*
>
> —HEBREWS 12:6

> *The adversary delights in using hardships and adversity to derail and detract God's people from being involved and effective in God's mission.*

> *Stay alert! Watch out for your great enemy, the devil. He prowls around like a roaring lion, looking for someone to devour. Stand firm against him, and be strong in your faith.*
>
> —1 PETER 5:8-9

Life's challenges reveal our weaknesses.

> *He delights in every detail of their lives [the godly].* —PSALM 37:23

> *My suffering was good for me, for it taught me to pay attention to your decrees.* —PSALM 119:71

> *God is ever-present with abundant resources and gives victory over life's trials.*

> *The Lord directs the steps of the godly. He delights in every detail of their lives. Though they stumble, they will never fall, for the Lord holds them by the hand.* —PSALM 37:23-24

> *But when I am afraid, I will put my trust in you. I praise God for what He has promised. I trust in God, so why should I be afraid? What can mere mortals do to me?* —PSALM 56:3-4

> *O God, you are my fortress...for you have been my refuge, a place of safety when I am in distress.*
>
> —PSALM 59:9,16

You have allowed me to suffer much hardship, but you will restore me to life again and lift me up from the depths of the earth. You will restore me to even greater honor and comfort me once again. —PSALM 71:20-21

So after you have suffered a little while, he will restore, support, and strengthen you, and he will place you on a firm foundation. —1 PETER 5:10

For I can do everything through Christ who gives me strength —PHILIPPIANS 4:13

For our present troubles are small and won't last very long. Yet they produce for us a glory that vastly outweighs them and will last forever. —2 CORINTHIANS 4:17

So now I am glad to boast in my weakness, so that the power of Christ can work through me. That's why I take pleasure in my weakness... and in the insults, hardships, persecutions, and troubles that I suffer for Christ. For when I am weak, then I am strong. —2 CORINTHIANS 12:9-10

Victory may or may not equate to removal of the hardship.

The Lord hears his people when they call to him for help. —PSALM 34:17

Though the Lord gave you adversity for food and suffering for drink, he will still be with you to teach you. —ISAIAH 30:20

We can rejoice, too, when we run into problems and trials, for we know that they help us develop endurance. And endurance develops strength of character, and character strengthens our confident hope of salvation. And this hope will not lead to disappointment. For we know how dearly God loves us. —ROMANS 5:3-5

You can patiently endure the same things we suffer. We are confident that as you share in our sufferings, you will also share in the comfort God gives us. —2 CORINTHIANS 1:6-7

God's is purposeful during times of adversity.

We can rejoice, too, when we run into problems and trials, for we know that they help us develop endurance. And endurance develops strength of character, and character strengthens our confident hope of salvation. And this hope will not lead to disappointment. For we know how dearly God loves us —ROMANS 5:3-5

My suffering was good for me, for it taught me to pay attention to your decrees. —PSALM 119:71

You must be content to trust God's character rather than your ability to understand. Suffering may be a test of trusting God for who He is, and not for what He does or allows.

Trust in the Lord with all your heart; do not depend on your own understanding.
—PROVERBS 3:5

No one can measure the depths of His [God's] understanding; He gives power to the weak and strength to the powerless...those that trust in the Lord will find new strength. They will soar high on wings like eagles. They will run and not grow weary. They will walk and not faint.
—ISAIAH 40:28,29,31

*The Lord is my strength and shield. I trust Him
with all my heart.* —PSALM 28:7

*But I am trusting you, O Lord, saying, 'You are
my God!' My future is in your hands.*
—PSALM 31:14-15

**God's peace is not the absence of tribulation, hardship, or
suffering; rather, it is his presence in the midst of tribulation.**

*I [Jesus] am leaving you with a gift—peace of
mind and heart. And the peace I give is a gift
the world cannot give. So don't be troubled or
afraid.* —JOHN 14:27

*I [Jesus] have told you all this so that you may
have peace in me. Here on earth you will have
many trials and sorrows. But take heart, because
I have overcome the world.* —JOHN 16:33

*Don't worry about anything; instead pray
about everything. Tell God what you need, and
thank Him for all He has done. Then you will
experience God's peace, which exceeds anything
we can understand. His peace will guard your
hearts and minds as you live in Christ Jesus.*
—PHILIPPIANS 4:6-7

**God is ever-present and loves you more than you will ever
realize!**

*For God loved the world so much that he gave his
one and only Son, so that everyone who believes
in him will not perish but have eternal life.*
—JOHN 3:16

*And the very hairs on your head are all numbered.
So don't be afraid; you are more valuable to God*

than a whole flock of sparrows. —LUKE 12:7

And I am convinced that nothing can ever separate us from God's love. Neither death nor life, neither angels nor demons, neither our fears for today nor our worries about tomorrow—not even the powers of hell can separate us from God's love. No power in the sky above or in the earth below—indeed, nothing in all creation will ever be able to separate us from the love of God that is revealed in Christ Jesus our Lord.

—ROMANS 8:38-39

I will always trust in God's unfailing love.

—PSALM 52:8

For His [God's] unfailing love toward those who fear him is as great as the height of the heavens above the earth. —PSALM 103:11

You [God] go before me and follow me...I can never escape your Spirit. I can never get away from your presence. —PSALM 139:5,7

The Good News: You Can Know God!

As mentioned, *Finding Strength in Tough Times* is written to present a Biblical and godly perspective to give readers understanding, hope, and helpful suggestions for dealing with hardship. It is possible, however, that some will not have a relationship with God. If this describes you, it's likely that much of the content will be difficult to understand or have any application in your life.

The Good News is that God loves you much more than you could ever imagine and has provided a solution to establish an eternal relationship with you. This relationship provides hope and assurance of your future while also giving you His supernatural strength and endurance for life's many adversities.

However, before presenting this "good news," it is helpful to understand the "bad news" that resulted in man's separation from God. Understanding this helps to appreciate what God has done and also reveals many of the shortcomings of various popular alternatives that the world offers.

How We Arrived Where We Are

The Bible tells us that in the beginning God created the world. God's creation was perfect and He proclaimed it as good. All was pure, and right. There was no pain, catastrophe, war, famine, conflict, and no sickness, tears, anger, or death. Man was perfect and had an eternal relationship with his perfect creator, God.

In God's perfection, He is 100 percent pure, just and loving. He will not and cannot have a relationship with anything that takes away from or dilutes His perfection; there are no exceptions. The Bible tells us that God's standard for a relationship is perfection. *"You are to be perfect, even as your Father in heaven is perfect,"* (Matthew 5:48).

Man, God's creation, was not created as a puppet. Man was created with the ability to make choices. This included the ability to think independently. God desired for man to choose to love, worship and obey Him. Anything less would not be genuine love.

Something happened that severed the relationship between God and man. Man chose to disobey God and do what was wrong. This was the first appearance of sin. The result of this disobedience was separation from God *"It's your sins that have cut you off from God. Because of your sins, He has turned away,"* (Isaiah 59:2). As said, a 100 percent perfect, pure, loving and just God cannot have a relationship with anything less. God and sin cannot co-exist together.

The relationship between God and man was broken. This separation from God caused by man's sin resulted in God's creation experiencing pain, hurt, wars, violence, and sickness, disease, and death that continues to the present.

The Problem

The resulting separation from God is a universal problem. It is a serious problem that applies to us all. Stated simply: how can imperfect, sinful people have a relationship with their perfect creator God?

This becomes even more problematic as the Bible tells us that no one meets God's requirement of perfection *"For everyone has sinned; we all fall short of God's glorious standard"* Romans 3:23; and, *"No one is righteous, not even one,"* (Romans 3:10). To restate the problem: if everyone is sinful, then how can anyone know and have a relationship with a perfectly just and loving God?

It's important that we understand "perfect justice" and "perfect love." Unlike our legal and court system that often blurs consequences, God's justice demands consequences for sinning. Perfect justice doesn't allow exceptions; anything short of perfect justice takes away from God's perfection. God's perfect love for man however moves Him to restore the broken relationship. Failure to respond dilutes God's perfect love. The two seem mutually exclusive and make any solution impossible—or does it?

A Review of Man's Solutions

At the core of evaluating any of the world's solutions is an understanding of God's holiness and His perfection. In the world's attempts to find its own pathway to God, God is redefined and becomes less than who He is, and, in this reshaping, becomes more like man.

Option 1: God is all-loving; He therefore should simply overlook man's sins.

Problem: While loving, this would make God less than just and no longer perfect. Sin has consequences and the consequence is death. *"For the wages of sin is death…"* (Romans 6:23); and *"For without the shedding of blood, there is no forgiveness"* (Hebrews 9:22). If God overlooked some or all sins, He would contradict the Bible and thus open the door for questioning God's attributes and the truth of the Scriptures.

Option 2: God should give man a list of conditions or criteria by which forgiveness can be earned and the eternal relationship with God would be restored.

Problem: Throughout history God has done this. The Old Testament is a series of man's attempts to follow God's rules; however, each time man failed to meet God's standards. Each time when God intervened and repeatedly gave man the option to obey, man rebelled. Man is incapable of living a sinless, perfect life. The Bible states a truth that applies to each one of us when it says, *"All have sinned and fall short"* (Romans 3:23).

Option 3: God should rank sins according to their severity with lesser sins forgiven or overlooked, and the "big" sins condemned that maintained the broken relationship.

Problem: This changes God's definition of sin and removes the consequences for some sins. If God overlooks sin regardless of how little or big in the eyes of man, God's perfection is negatively impacted. God's thoughts and standards are dramatically different from those of the world. God's good is perfection; man's good is relative, circumstantial, and defined by man. Regardless of how "good" a person might be, any sin contaminates God's perfection and makes a relationship impossible. God doesn't grade on the curve.

Option 4: Create a balance sheet for life; if the "good" outweighs the "bad" in a person's life then God should accept the person and restore the relationship.

Problem: Similar to Option 3, this dilutes the definition of sin and takes away from God's perfection by accepting anything "bad." This option also glorifies man since such an alternative presents man with an opportunity to "earn" salvation by good works and results in pride. The Bible tells us that it is impossible to "earn" a relationship with God based upon what we do. *"Salvation is not a reward for the good things we have done, so none of us can boast about it."* (Ephesians 2:9)

Option 5: God should make the basis of a relationship upon family history. If one's family, past or present, is a Christian, or one who attends church and lives a good life, then that's suitable for all other family members in God's sight.

Problem: This doesn't deal with individual sins and takes away from God's standards of having a relationship only with individual perfection. An individual relationship with God does not come by a proxy family member or friend.

Option 6: God's criteria for a relationship should be based on intellectually acknowledging and "believing in God."

Problem: This problem is with the definition of "believe." The Bible tells us that,*"even the demons believe in God"* (James 2:19). While believing in God is essential, it is a belief that goes much deeper beyond simple acknowledgement or assent that God exists. It is one that includes personally accepting, adhering to, relying upon, trusting in, confessing, and accepting what God has done to restore the relationship. Intellectual acknowledgement, by itself, is unacceptable absent this personal dimension of "belief." One can believe a ladder exists without ever stepping up onto the ladder. Relationship belief with God requires "stepping up His ladder."

Option 7: The Bible tells us that the penalty for sin is death (Romans 6:23). Therefore, God should accept the sacrifice of another person for our sins.

Problem: While this option is farfetched today, primitive societies practiced this option to appease their "gods." However, such human sacrifices have no place in Christianity. Notwithstanding the horror of selecting a person, the human sacrifice would have to be perfect and sinless. No such person exists, and sinful man already has a "death sentence" apart from God. Everyone is sinful; therefore no such perfect sacrifice exists. Therefore the sacrifice is tainted and unacceptable. (This option is only mentioned as some fail to recognize the significant difference as explained below in the sacrifice of Jesus as opposed to any other human acts of sacrifice.)

Option 8: God should recognize that all "ways" to Him end up in the same place and one is as good as any other. There are many religions in the world that claim to establish a relationship with God. Following one or several of them is just as good as Christianity.

Problem: This option is typically referred to as the "mountain analogy." There are many paths up the mountain, but they all end up in the same place. This option finds favor with many and follows the world's message of practicing tolerance. There are even new religions (such as the Baha'i faith) appearing that ascribe to a total synthesis of all world religions into one unified belief. Tolerance has become the license to ignore truth and minimize the glaring differences in various "paths" up the mountain. How can anyone endorse all religions as the same apart from any knowledge of the history and each one's core beliefs? Some deny the existence of any personal God and a life after death, while others subscribe in their so-called holy writings to the killing of non-believers and label them as enemies. Truth is truth and one cannot practice reductionism by ignoring any religion's core beliefs and assigning them as non-essentials.

This option is contrary to the Bible that clearly teaches that there is only one way to God and that is through His way that He has provided. Most other religions fail to deal with the consequences of sin and are based on man earning or achieving some degree of a relationship with God. Their focus is on man and not God. These are false and contrary to Biblical teaching. *"Jesus told him, 'I am the way, the truth, and the life. No one can come to the Father except through Me'"* (John 14:6).

God's Option and His Good News

God, Himself, would provide the perfect sacrifice for sin. God, would take upon Himself the form of a man [Jesus], live a perfect life, and allow Himself to be sacrificed. *"Though He [Jesus] was God, He did not think equality with God as something to cling to. Instead, He gave up His divine privileges, He took the humble position of a slave and was born a human being. When He appeared in human form, He humbled Himself in obedience* to God and die a criminal's death on a cross. Therefore, God elevated Him to the place of highest honor and gave Him the name above all other names" (Philippians 2:6-9).

Jesus was the only acceptable substitute and payment, once and for all, for man's sins. Then His visible resurrection was visible proof of meeting God's standards. Jesus' sacrifice demonstrated victory over death and eternal life. What man couldn't do, Jesus did for us.

God now offers His Son's act as a gift to whoever personally believes what Jesus did, and trusts in Jesus as their personal Savior. *"For God loved the world so much that He gave His one and only Son, so that everyone who believes in Him will not perish but have eternal life,* (John 3:16).

Restoring the relationship with God is then done by one prayerfully confessing that he or she is a sinner, asking God for forgiveness by taking and receiving His Son, Jesus, as his or her personal Savior.

God assures us that once this is done that our sins, past, present, and future, are forgiven, not remembered, and we have a lifelong, eternal relationship with Him based upon all He has done for us in His son, Jesus. The relationship is restored and accomplished only by God, not us.

God's option is without problem. His perfect love and justice were served. God's love was satisfied, as He loved us so much that He gave His only Son; God's justice was served via a perfect sinless sacrifice. His solution is perfect.

If there is any problem, it is with man's pride and tendency to postpone submitting to God, accepting what He has done, and confessing Jesus as Lord and Savior. The Bible is clear about what awaits us all in Hebrews 9:27, "And just as each person is destined to die once and after that comes judgment, so also Jesus Christ died once for all as a sacrifice to take away the sins of many people."

Psalms 119:39 is instructive and timely, "I pondered the direction of my life and I turned to follow Your [God's] ways." Is it possible that God has allowed hardship to come into your life to cause you to turn to Him? As mentioned before, God created us with the ability to choose.

My prayer is that you will act upon God's good news and His invitation to establish an eternal relationship. The Bible tells us that if we will confess with our mouth that Jesus is Lord and believe in your heart that God raised Him from the dead, you will be saved (Romans 10:9).

Choose now to come to your heavenly Father.

I also offer a simple prayer that can put into your own words.

Father God, I confess that I am far from perfect
and am a sinner.

I believe in what You did for me in Your Son, Jesus.

Father, I want to accept Your Son, Jesus, as my Savior.

Thank You for sending Jesus and forgiving me.

Thank You for receiving me and now coming into my life.

Father, help me to grow in knowing You.

I pray this based upon what You have done by Jesus,
in His name,

Amen

Outline and References for God's Plan:

1. All have sinned

    Romans 3:23

    1 John 1:8-10

    James 2:10

2. Two certainties: Death and Judgment

    Hebrews 9:27

3. Wages of sin is death

    Romans 6:23

4. There is no forgiveness without sacrificial blood

    Hebrews 9:22

5. Jesus Christ died as payment for our sins

    1 Peter 2:24 and 3:18

6. Sins forgiven and not remembered

    Hebrews 10:17-18

    Psalms 103-10-11

7. Saved by grace gift and not works

    Ephesians 2:8-9

    Galatians 2:21

8. God is ready to enter your life

    Revelation 3:20

    Romans 10:13

9. Invitation to confess and believe

          Romans 10:9

          John 3:16

10. Believe and be assured you have eternal life

          1 John 5:11-13

          John 1:12

11. Permanence of God's love

          Romans 8:38-39

12. Security of the believer

          John 10:28-29

          Titus 3:5

          Romans 5:8-10

          Ephesians 1:13

          2 Timothy 1:12

          Hebrews 7:25

God's Forgiveness of Sins:

- He removes sin as far as East is from West. (Psalms 102:12)
- He cleanses and removes stain from sin. (Isaiah 1:18)
- He completely puts sin behind Him. (Isaiah 38:17)
- He remembers sins no more. (Jeremiah 31:34)
- He stomps our sins underfoot. (Micah 7:19)
- He casts our sins in depths of sea. (Micah 7:19)
- He is faithful to forgive our sins. (1 John 1:9)
- He cleanses us from all unrighteousness. (1 John 1:9)
- He gives mercy and grace at time of need. (Hebrews 4:16)

- His sacrifice was once and for all. (Hebrews 7:27)
- No longer any need for sin offerings. (Hebrews 10:18)
- Jesus has perfected us forever. (Hebrews 10:14)
- We are justified by Jesus' one act. (Romans 5:18)
- No condemnation for those in Christ. (Romans 8:1)

ENDNOTES

1 Internet, "Interview with Rick Warren by Paul Bradshaw," www.southasianconnection.com, April 28, 2005

2 Ventura County Star; Terry Mattingly, Religion, B4; March 21, 2009

3 Charles Colson, *Loving God* (Grand Rapids: Zondervan Publishing House, 1983), 218

4 Eugene Peterson, *Living The Message* (New York: HarperCollins, 1996), 181

5 A.W. Tozer, *That Incredible Christian* (Harrisburg, Pa: Christian Publishing, Inc., 1964), 27

6 A.W. Tozer, *The Knowledge of the Holy* (New York: Harper and Bros, 1961), 10

7 Henry and Richard Blackaby, Spiritual Leadership (Nashville: Broadman & Holman Publishing, 2001), 41-42

8 A.W. Tozer, *The Pursuit of God* (Camp Hill, Pa: Christian Publications, Inc., 1982), 16-17

9 John Piper, *The Legacy of the Sovereign Joy* (Wheaton: Crossway Books, Good News Publishers, 2000), 70

10 John H. Sammis, 1887, Public Domain

11 A.W. Tozer, *The Pursuit of God* (Camp Hill, Pa: Christian Publications, Inc., 1982), 16-17

12 Dr. Richard Blackaby, The CEO Forum member devotionals (Colorado Springs, Colo: The CEO Forum, November, 2008)

13 Sally Breedlove, *Choosing Rest* (Colorado Springs, Colorado: Navpress, 2002), 98-99

14 Dr. James Dobson, *When God Doesn't Make Sense* (Wheaton, Illinois: Tyndale House Publishers, 1993), 59

15 John R.W. Stott, *Basic Christianity* (Downers Grove, Illinois, Inter-Varsity Press, 1958, 1971), 140-141

16 Dr. Ed Murphy, *Handbook For Spiritual Warfare* (Nashville: Thomas Nelson, 1997), 1

17 Charles Spurgeon, *The Sword and the Trowel* (London: London Metrop Tabernacle, Biblio Bazaar, 2010), 24

18 J. Oswald Sanders, *Spiritual Leadership* (Chicago: The Moody Bible Institute of Chicago, 1967), 142-143

19 Robert Louis Stevenson, 1850-1894 (Thinkexist.com; historical famous quote resource)

20 Francis A Schaeffer, *The Great Evangelical Disaster* (Westchester, Illinois: Crossway Books, 1984), 29

21 Henry and Richard Blackaby, *Spiritual Leadership* (Nashville: Broadman & Holman Publishing, 2001), 5

22 Mark Twain, *The Adventures of Huckleberry Finn* (New York: Barnes & Noble Books, 2003), 13-14

23 J.B. Phillips, *Your God Is Too Small* (New York: MacMillan Publishing Co, Inc., 1961), title

24 Elisabeth Elliot, *The World Must Be Shown, Keep A Quiet Heart* (Back To The Bible devotionals; November 17, 2009)

25 John R. Stott, *Understanding Christ* (Grand Rapids: Zondervan Publishing House, 1981), 143

26 The Navigators, *Design For Discipleship* (Colorado Springs, Colo: NavPress Publishing Co., 1973,1980,2006), DFD2, pg. 42

27 Jerry Bridges, *Trusting God* (Colorado Springs, Colorado, Navpress, 1988), 175

28 Joni and Friends Ministry, The Christian Post, June 26, 2010

ACKNOWLEDGMENTS

To even suggest that *Finding Strength in Tough Times* is the work of one individual would be a gross misrepresentation. It is the product of many willing to share their experiences; relive their hurts; identify what helped them during their respective painful times; and all who gave encouragement and suggestions for the book's improvement.

Special thanks and acknowledgement must go to:

Jim and Kortni Duff who, over three years, encouraged and challenged me continuously to take this work down from the shelf, dust it off, and continue writing (all the while giving me lessons in grammar and punctuation). Their support ensured this book would make it into the public arena.

Kevin and Rrachel Fitzpatrick, close friends and a loving Christian couple, who with their weekly Bible Study, field-tested and edited the content and provided continuous valuable feedback.

Fred Force, a longtime mentor, Bible scholar, and Christian brother, who checked the validity of the many Scriptural principles and offered many outstanding suggestions.

Bob and Fran Martin, longtime precious friends, counselors and, followers of Christ, who reviewed the developing work and tested the content with their friends, study group and counselees.

Noel and Sandy Funderburk, who provided helpful suggestions and examples on how to manage tough times as exhibited in their own lives and with many others.

John and DeeDee Davidson, close friends who not only provided encouragement but also shared their experiences of dealing with adversity victoriously.

Dr. Richard Blackaby, Blackaby Ministries International, and Mac McQuiston, Steve Menefee, Larry Collett, Rich Case, Steve South, and Berry Carter along with all The CEO Forum members who ministered to me personally through the Spiritual Leadership Institute providing helpful Biblical concepts for victims of adversity.

My Pastor Steve Larson, and his wife, Connie, close friends, who regularly provided valuable insight and opened my eyes to ways of ministering to those experiencing adversity while filling my spiritual "tank" each Sunday with sound Biblical teaching.

And, of course, none of this ever would have come to fruition without the wonderful Anna McHargue, Senior Editor, Russell Media, who repeatedly worked her editing magic and ever-so-gently pushed me to adhere to a rigorous schedule of deadlines all the while lamenting over the evil BCS football empire and praising her esteemed Boise State Broncos.

And, certainly, to my wonderful wife of fifty years, Saundra (Soni), who painstakingly read countless versions and offered suggestions while demonstrating loving patience and understanding as I retreated and disappeared regularly to write. She's truly a co-author and embodies the Scriptural truth in Proverbs 31 when speaking of a model wife by saying, "She is more precious than rubies." Soni is that and so much more!

Visit Russell Media for our latest offerings:

www.russell-media.com